TRANS ALLYSHIP WORKBOOK

Building Skills to Support Trans People in Our Lives

BY DAVEY SHLASKO
Illustrated by Kai Hofius

Madison, Wisconsin · 2017

TRANS ALLYSHIP WORKBOOK

Building Skills to Support Trans People in Our Lives

THINK AGAIN

ILLUSTRATIONS BY KAI HOFIUS

PUBLISHED BY THINK AGAIN TRAINING
MADISON, WI

The previous edition, titled *Trans★ Ally Workbook: Getting Pronouns Right and What It Teaches Us About Gender*, was published in 2014 by Think Again Training, then based in Oakland, CA. Most of the content of Chapter 4, including the sections "What are Pronouns?," "Why Pronouns Matter," and "Barriers to Getting Pronouns Right, and How to Overcome Them" are drawn from that edition with only minor updates.

"How Using They as a Singular Pronoun Can Change the World" was originally published on Feministing.com in February, 2015.

Thanks to many people who provided their personal insights and editorial feedback on this book and the earlier edition, including:

SOPHIE ARGETSINGER, CHRIS BARCELOS, RACHEL BRIGGS, CHASE CATALANO, KENDRA COLBURN, SUMMER CORRIE, CIAN DALZEL, JONAH ALINE DANIEL, TOBIAS K. DAVIS, ILANA GERJUOY, SONNY GRAVES, KATJA HAHN D'ERRICO, ERIC HAMAKO, SARAH HERSHEY, KAI HOFIUS, RAMESH KATHNANDA, JOANNA KENT KATZ, DANE KUTTLER, NELL MYHAND, SELE NADEL-HAYES, LIORA O'DONNELL GOLDENSHER, CAMILLE ROBERTSON, ERIN SEGAL, MARGARET SHLASKO, NORMA SMITH, SHANNON WAY, AND E ZOLLI

TABLE OF CONTENTS

INTRODUCTION

ALLYSHIP (n.): *Informed, accountable action that contributes to other people's ability to survive and thrive in a context of inequality.*

THE AIM OF THIS BOOK is to help you get better at understanding and supporting trans people in your community. Maybe you have a trans friend, relative or colleague, and want to make sure you're being as welcoming and supportive as possible. Maybe you learned from a news story about challenges that trans people face, and want to do your part to be part of the solution. Maybe you're a teacher or service provider, witnessing firsthand how trans students and community members are not always served well by institutions that are meant to help them.

Whatever your motivation, you're not alone. Trans people have become more visible in mainstream media and communities, yet remain vulnerable to discrimination and violence. Many people are aware of this and looking for ways to be a better ally. This book is for you.

This book is also for trans people like me, who want to be better allies to other trans people whose experiences differ from our own. Trans communities are diverse, and what each of us needs from our allies can vary widely. The kinds of support and acknowledgment that feel good to, say, a trans woman military veteran in her sixties are likely to be very different than what feels good to a nonbinary fourteen-year-old high school student. What works for someone who is newly exploring their trans identity will be different than what works for someone who transitioned decades ago. What makes sense for someone whose gender is honored in their indigenous culture may be different than what makes sense for someone whose gender bucks their culture's expectations. Even as we are often called upon to teach our friends and loved ones (and unfortunately, our teachers and therapists and doctors) how to be the allies we need, we should remember that we are also learners, and keep working to be better allies to each other.

This book is not meant to teach you how to be an activist for trans rights—although it might help, if activism is part of your life. Participating in trans movements is super important, and allies can play vital roles. Many brilliant trans leaders and organizations are publishing work on trans movement strategy (see for example Reina Gossett, Dean Spade,

Southerners On New Ground [SONG], Transgender Law Center, Sylvia Rivera Law Project, Gender Justice League and others) and you should absolutely go learn from them. This book is about the personal stuff—how we go about our days in communities and organizations where trans people are marginalized, in a way that helps trans people survive and thrive. It's about how we make sure that our best intentions of being welcoming and supportive actually translate into action that comes across that way.

The first edition of this book came out about three and a half years ago. Since then, we have seen a dramatic increase in the visibility of trans people in mainstream media and communities in the U.S. Politically active trans celebrities like Laverne Cox and Janet Mock are widely known even outside LGBTQ communities, unlike most trans leaders and artists of previous decades. Non-famous trans people are visible as both authors and subjects of mainstream media in widely-read outlets like the Huffington Post and the New York Times.

This visibility is recent, but it was made possible by decades of advocacy and struggle. Trans activists and our allies have successfully lobbied for legal protections against discrimination in some states, along with more realistic requirements for those who want to change the gender on their government-issued ids. In the medical realm, acceptance is slowly growing for a more patient-centered approach to transition-related medical care. Many schools, human service agencies, and businesses now understand that training their staff to work respectfully and effectively with trans people is an important part of their overall diversity and inclusion efforts. Each of these successes enables greater visibility, and greater visibility brings further positive change even closer.

Unfortunately, visibility also has some downsides. At the same time as sympathetic news stories about trans folks (especially trans children) have ballooned, reports of violent attacks against trans people, especially trans women of color, have also skyrocketed. It's hard to tell how much this reflects an increase in violence as opposed to an increase in attention to the violence that has always been rampant. But it's not hard to imagine that some people who hold bigoted feelings against trans people might feel more motivated to act on those feelings after seeing news stories about trans people living, working, and going to school in their communities. On a political level, we've seen aggressive and ill-informed anti-trans initiatives that seek to prevent trans people from using public restrooms, from changing the gender category on our identity documents, from accessing usable health insurance, and more.

Another downside of the increase in media attention is that much of the media coverage is oversimplified, disrespectful, or just lazy journalism. It tends to focus repetitively on a few stereotyped kinds of stories, like the innocent trans child who has "always known," or the "first trans _____" who is ostensibly breaking barriers by holding a particular kind of job. Many of these news stories emphasize the reporter's naivety, confusion or amazement. Trans issues are portrayed as new, complicated, or scandalous, with the effect of exoticizing situations that are (for better or worse) totally ordinary in trans life. Such coverage may leave you knowing less than you did before about how to talk to and about trans people respectfully. Meanwhile, other, more nuanced trans stories remain untold.

So how do we go about becoming better allies? In the trans inclusion trainings I provide for teachers, human services providers, and communities, I strive to balance two important goals: On one hand, I want people to really "get it" about what it means to be trans—to understand both intellectually and emotionally who trans people are and what we might need in order to survive and thrive in a society that marginalizes us. On the other hand, whether or not they "get it," I want people to know what to do and say (and just as importantly, what *not* to do and say) in order to welcome trans people they encounter. Of course, the more you "get it," the more doing and saying the right thing will come naturally. But that deeper kind of learning takes time, so sometimes you have to "fake it 'til you make it"—do the right thing even if you don't yet understand exactly why it's right.

In this book, I've tried to strike the same balance. Some sections focus on "getting it," mostly by explaining trans identities and experiences and offering opportunities for reflection. Other sections focus on concrete actions you can take to support trans individuals and communities. Throughout, you'll find practical and reflective exercises you can use to hone your allyship. I encourage you to work on both the practical and the conceptual, but feel free to start with whatever section feels most useful to you. Most sections will make sense even out of order. When you've taken in the pieces that feel most urgent, you can come back to explore the rest.

Throughout the book, I mention publications and organizations that you can turn to for further information. These are listed, along with even more resources, in the resource list beginning on p. 91.

A quick note on terminology: The language we use to talk about trans issues is constantly evolving. Brief definitions are provided throughout the book for words that may be new to many readers, and there is a glossary at the end with more extensive explanations. People use these terms in a variety of ways, and their usage has changed and will continue to change over time. Terminology also varies regionally, so this book is most directly relevant to readers in the U.S., although readers in other English-speaking places have also found it useful. When referring to an individual's identity, it's more important to understand what that person means by the terms they use, rather than to memorize the "standard" definitions.

CHAPTER ONE: *What is Allyship?*

In the most general sense, allyship means helping each other out, or working together—being in alliance. In the context of social justice activism, it means supporting someone (or some group) who is impacted by oppression or inequality differently than you are. Sometimes allyship refers specifically to people with a particular, privileged identity, supporting people who do not share that privilege—for example, straight people who work for LGB (lesbian, gay and bisexual) rights or white people who support racial justice movements. Other times, allyship can include people within the group—like trans people seeking to support trans people who are different from ourselves. Sometimes allyship refers to an attitude—such as believing that people should not be discriminated against—and other times it requires more active engagement.

When ally is used to refer to an attitude, the term can become so watered down that it doesn't mean much and even becomes counterproductive. Activists and scholars have written about the problems that arise when people can become so attached to their ally "identity" that they defend it even at the expense of the people they claim to be in alliance with. If you want to read more about that, Mia McKenzie's blog *Black Girl Dangerous*, and her book of the same name, are great places to start.

For the purpose of this book, being an ally is not something you are, nor something you think or feel, but something you *do*. It is informed, accountable action that contributes to other people's ability to survive and thrive in a context of inequality. You can be an ally to a group or to an individual.

I often use Dr. Barbara Love's essay "Developing a Liberatory Consciousness" to explore the ingredients required for effective allyship. Love talks about awareness, analysis, accountability, and action.

Awareness means developing the capacity to notice when something is wrong—to notice when someone is being excluded, insulted or discriminated against. In the dominant culture, marginalization of trans people is so pervasive that it can be hard to notice because it just seems normal. In particular, many of the barriers trans people face are not a result of deliberate discrimination (although there's plenty of that, too) but rather of systems that are set up on the assumption that trans people don't exist. Forms that require you to check off male or female, public restrooms that are designated for men and women with no other options, and the overall absence of trans people in books, movies and television are all examples that allies should cultivate the ability to notice, along with more overt violence and discrimination. In order to develop that awareness, we need to be at least somewhat familiar with the diversity of trans identities and experiences that exist.

Awareness also means becoming conscious of our own beliefs, feelings, and assumptions about trans people and about gender in general. This allows us to make more conscious decisions and to act on our actual values, rather than on stereotypes we have absorbed without even noticing them. Chapter 4, "Getting Pronouns Right and What it Teaches Us About Gender," is mostly about developing this kind of self-awareness.

Analysis refers to developing a nuanced understanding of what we know and observe. Beyond noticing when something is wrong or right, analysis requires us to think through why and how those things are happening, what is wrong or right about them, and why it matters. It also requires us to make connections between different kinds of events, beliefs, and systems. An *analysis* of challenges trans people face in the world can help to explain what male/female check boxes have to do with family violence against trans youth. It can highlight how some current tensions within trans communities are entangled with the legacy of the medical system's pathologizing approach to trans identity. It can strengthen coalitions by clarifying how police departments use some of the same tools (such as special enforcement zones) to target communities of color and trans communities, or how politicians use transphobia to drum up support for bills that hurt poor people, people of color, and people with disabilities along with trans people.

Action simply means doing stuff—in this case, doing stuff that has a positive effect on a trans individual or community. Your allyship can't be all in your head. You may start out with reflection and self-education, but if you don't eventually move to taking action, then your project is one of self-improvement more than allyship. Action can be as small as accompanying your trans friend in a public restroom to shield them from harassment, and as large as organizing a campaign to change a law that hurts trans people. Chapter 5, "Allyship in Action," is about some of the many ways you can take action as a trans ally.

Finally, *accountability* is about relationships. Who do we trust to give us accurate feedback about how we're doing as an ally? Whose work do we look to for direction in setting priorities for action? If you're focusing on being an ally to a particular trans person, you are accountable to that person. That means you recognize that they, not you, are the ultimate authority on what kind of self-education and action you should be prioritizing as their ally. But you can also form relationships of accountability with other trans people in your life, and with other skilled allies, so that you aren't only relying on someone you're trying to support to teach you how to support them. You can even have indirect relationships of accountability with trans authors and organizations, who can help you develop your awareness and analysis and provide some guidance about appropriate allyship behaviors.

In fact, allies should always be accountable to trans communities and movements beyond the individual(s) we're supporting, so that we don't accidentally undermine some trans people while trying to support others. For example, it may be helpful in some contexts to reassure a trans person that you don't see their trans identity as a mental illness, even though the medical model has historically understood it this way. Many trans people would agree that trans identity should not be pathologized (understood as an illness). But when you say that someone's trans identity is acceptable *because* it is not a mental illness, there's an unintended consequence of reinforcing the stigma attached to mental illness, which undermines the ability of trans and cisgender people with mental illness to survive and thrive.

For trans people seeking to be in alliance with each other, it is important to remember that what works best for us does not necessarily work best for all trans people. Being in relationships of accountability with other trans folks whose identities and experiences are different from our own can not only make us better at supporting each other, but also help us to explain things to our cisgender allies in a way that doesn't leave anyone out.

CISGENDER: Not trans.

Reflection: The 4 As of Liberatory Consciousness

Consider Barbara Love's 4 elements of a liberatory consciousness: Awareness, Analysis, Action and Accountability. Take stock of your own allyship to trans people. How are you doing on each of the four elements? Where do you have room for growth?

Reflection: Relationships of Accountability

What are your relationships of accountability around trans allyship? Make a list of individuals you know personally, individuals you follow on social media, authors whose work you look to, and organizations whose leadership you trust around trans issues.

Review your list of people, and ask yourself: How many of the individuals are trans? Do they include a balance of people with nonbinary identities, trans women, and trans men? Do they include people of different ages, races, class backgrounds, professions and experiences? Do they include people who have been "out" as trans for a long time, along with those who have come out or transitioned more recently? Do they include people who live with disabilities, people who have been (or are still) incarcerated, people who have been (or are still) homeless?

Now look at the organizations on your list. Who do these organizations represent? Who is in leadership? What is the balance (within each organization, and also across all the organizations on your list) of leadership by and for trans people of a variety of genders, ages, races, classes, and experiences? Additionally, consider the organizations' relationships: What other organizations do they collaborate with? What is their reputation in trans communities, especially among trans folks who are poor, people of color, and/or otherwise marginalized?

What patterns do you notice? What sorts of voices might be missing from your accountability network?

Finally, make a plan to fill those gaps. Perhaps start with the resource list at the end of this book, and/or with some of the trans authors mentioned throughout the book. Find out what your local trans communities and organizations are working on, and consider building in-person relationships through volunteering or attending discussion groups. Aspire to have at least two "real life" relationships of accountability with people who are different from you and each other.

CHAPTER TWO:
What is Trans, and Who are Trans People?

In order to understand what trans encompasses and who trans people are, we first have to understand what gender is and isn't.

Very broadly, gender is a system of categorizing people according to factors like anatomy, identity, appearance, and mannerisms, and attributing meaning to those categories. Different cultures have different gender systems in terms of what gender categories are acknowledged (men, women, and other categories), the meanings attached to the categories (gender roles, stereotypes and expectations), and which factors (anatomy, identity, etc.) are most important in determining someone's category. If you're interested in exploring gender diversity across cultures, Serena Nanda's book *Gender Diversity: Crosscultural Variations* is a great place to start. (However, be aware that Nanda uses some academic/anthropology jargon that's considered out of date and disrespectful by many trans people).

For people who have grown up in the dominant US culture—even if it wasn't the only culture we grew up in—some aspects of this gender system are so pervasive that they seem natural and inevitable. And yet, they don't reflect the diversity of gender experiences that people have. So it's important to dig into what gender *isn't*:

Gender isn't binary, although most of us have been taught to think of it that way. *Binary* simply means that something has only two categories, like on/off or yes/no. The *binary gender system* is the way of thinking that says there are exactly two kinds of people in the world—men and women. It assumes that there are no categories or experiences of gender beyond men and women—no one who's both, neither, on a spectrum between, or something else entirely—and that which category you belong to says everything anyone needs to know about your gender.

> BINARY GENDER SYSTEM: The set of ideas and structures that assume and reinforce a two-category system of gender (men/women).

In addition to a way of thinking, the binary gender system also includes concrete structures that sort and confine people into gender categories. M/F check boxes, public restrooms labeled for men and women, and sex-segregated shelters, jails and hospital wards all are part of the binary gender system. Even if we personally don't believe in the *ideas* behind the binary gender system, these *structures* can still have a significant impact on our lives.

SEXUAL ORIENTATION

- *sexual attraction*
- *emotional attraction*
- *sexual behaviors*
- *partnership decisions*
- *identity*
- *community*

GENDER EXPRESSION
Behaviors that express, or can be interpreted as expressing, something about gender.

GENDER IDENTITY
One's understanding of oneself in relation to concepts like man, woman, trans, genderqueer, and many others.

ASSIGNED SEX
Gender category for ID documents and other administrative systems.

BIOLOGICAL SEX
Includes genotype, internal and external sex organs, hormone levels, secondary sex characteristics, etc.

The genderbread cookie is an image that many educators and activists use to communicate key concepts related to gender. The earliest version I have found or heard of was developed by youth leaders at the Sexual Minority Youth Resource Center in Portland, OR, around 1997. In 1998, activists with the Trans Activist Network in Western Massachusetts (later the Western Massachusetts chapter of the Massachusetts Transgender Political Coalition, MTPC) printed a version of it in a training guide; this was cited in the first published version, in a chapter in *Teaching for Diversity and Social Justice, 2nd edition*, in 2007. The genderbread cookie was always meant to be shared and adapted freely by educators and activists who use it, and this has continued to happen. There are many versions in circulation, with different strengths and weaknesses. However, one user—the proprietor of the website itspronouncedmetrosexual.com—falsely claimed to have authored it, effectively plagiarizing and privatizing what should be an evolving community resource. And his version isn't even that good, in that it still relies pretty heavily on binary logic. Please don't use it, and don't credit him with inventing the genderbread! The version presented here is my current adaptation, based on what works well with training groups I work with. Anyone is free to use and adapt it, crediting me as the author of this version (not of the whole idea).

The binary gender system lumps together several different aspects of human experience: biological sex, assigned sex, gender identity, and gender expression. Actually, these are all different from each other—and none of them are binary.

Biological sex refers to features of one's body including genitals, internal reproductive organs, chromosomes, and hormone levels, along with secondary sex characteristics like body hair, facial hair, fat-to-muscle ratio, breast development and vocal pitch. Even at a biological level, sex is not binary.

Intersex people are people whose bodies are not easily categorized as simply male or female. Sometimes this is apparent at birth, and other times not until puberty. There are many different reasons a person's body might be difficult to categorize, ranging from unusual chromosomes (e.g. rather than XX or XY, people can have XXY, XXX, XO, or a mixture of different sex chromosomes in different cells), to hormone levels that differ from population averages, to genital anatomy that doesn't look like what we're used to.

> INTERSEX: Describes people whose bodies are not easily categorized as simply male or female.

Depending on how you count, anywhere from one in 2000 to one in 60 people are intersex. In some cases, the features that make a body hard to categorize also cause health problems, but in most cases they do not, and the only "problem" is the difficulty that other people have in categorizing the person. Intersex people often face significant stigma and mistreatment in the medical system. For example, until recently it was standard practice to operate on intersex babies' genitals to make them look more "normal,"

> Intersex people used to be referred to as *hermaphrodites*. Now this term is seen as inaccurate and offensive. It's inaccurate because in biology, hermaphrodite usually refers to animals that have complete male and female sex organs, such as earth worms. Although some intersex people have both ovarian and testicular tissue, there is no such thing as a human who is a true hermaphrodite in that sense. The term hermaphrodite also refers to a character in Greek mythology—Hermaphroditus, a male god who became physically fused to a female water nymph. Many people find it offensive to refer to real humans as if they are mythical beings. Finally, the word hermaphrodite as a medical diagnosis has a lot of negative baggage because of how it has been used to pathologize and mistreat intersex people. Intersex is a more neutral and respectful term.

even though it is rarely medically necessary and often harms the person's sexual or reproductive functioning. Intersex activists, working through organizations like InterACT, have worked to end unnecessary infant genital surgeries and improve how intersex people are treated in the medical system.

Even among people who are not intersex, bodies can have a wide range of male and female sex characteristics. Some people whose bodies are easily categorized as female have tiny breasts or deep voices; some people whose bodies are easily categorized as male have significant breast tissue or barely any facial hair. In fact, the features we associate with maleness and femaleness are partially based on dominant culture stereotypes and beauty norms, which are not only sexist but also racist, ageist, sizeist and more. Take facial hair, for example. When someone whose body is easily categorized as female goes through menopause and grows coarse chin hairs, does that person become less female? Or does it make more sense to just say that this is part of the spectrum of what female can look like? To add another layer of complication, many people of East Asian descent whose bodies are easily categorized as male do not grow much facial hair, while many people from Southwest Asia/North Africa (the "Middle East") whose bodies are easily categorized as female do. This is just part of the range of how maleness and femaleness can show up, and no more or less normal than the dominant culture norms demanding that female bodies be slender, curvy and hairless while male bodies be large, muscled, and hairy.

Rather than two entirely separate categories, it can be useful to think of maleness and femaleness as a collection of spectrums—a spectrum of breast development, another of genital development, another of testosterone levels, another of estrogen levels, another of X and Y chromosomes, etc.—some of which change over the course of someone's life, and all of which interact in immensely complex ways.

Often when people say *biological sex*, they actually mean *assigned sex* (also called *sex assigned at birth*). Assigned sex is the legal/administrative category—almost always male or female—to which babies are assigned at birth based on the appearance of the external genitals. This category is recorded on our medical record, birth certificate, and social security record, and becomes required information every time we apply for a government-issued ID, request government funding (like food stamps or federal student loans), and when we enroll in

> SEX ASSIGNED AT BIRTH: The legal/administrative category—almost always male or female—to which babies are assigned at birth based on the appearance of the external genitals.

school. That categorization as male or female is always a drastic oversimplification of the maleness and/or femaleness of our bodies.

Gender identity refers to someone's internal sense of self, as related to gender categories like man, woman, boy, girl, and many others. It too is not binary. Some people identify not as a man or a woman but as both, neither, in between, or beyond the two categories. Some people with nonbinary gender identities find that the language that would describe their genders doesn't really exist yet, and so new terms have proliferated in the past few decades. Genderqueer, nonbinary, enby (from nb, short for nonbinary), gender-fluid, and agender are all words coined since 1990 to name different kinds of nonbinary gender identity (and defined in the glossary).

> GENDER IDENTITY: Refers to someone's internal sense of self in terms of the gender categories they have access to, like man, woman, boy, girl, and many others.

But nonbinary gender identity is not new. Throughout history many, if not most, cultures have had more than two gender categories. Most cultures have two main gender categories (like men and women), and many have one or more additional categories that are considered unusual, but not abnormal, ways to be. Hijra in South Asia, Fa'afafine in Samoa, Mahu in Hawaii, Muxe in Oaxaca, and the various Two Spirit traditions in indigenous North America, are all examples of traditional gender categories beyond man and woman. Some of these terms are still in wide use. Other traditions have been obscured or distorted by the violence of colonization and cultural domination, and are being recovered by activists within those communities who identify with the category.

Sometimes, people are tempted to claim a traditional gender category from a culture that's not part of their heritage. It might feel validating to know that a culture has/had a word for people "like" you, when your own culture and the dominant culture don't have words for it. But this kind of claiming is a form of cultural appropriation, and many indigenous people find it offensive and harmful to the communities where the terms originate. Kai Minov's essay on the *Black Girl Dangerous* blog, "Why Non-Natives Appropriating 'Two-Spirit' Hurts," provides a really important perspective on this. For people with nonbinary gender identities, being allies to each other must include understanding and respecting how cultural and historical context, including the context of colonization, make gender traditions and gender experiences specific.

Most people experience their gender identity as relatively stable over the course of their life—more stable than, say, their hobbies or their fashion sense. Some people experience their gender identity as shifting one or more times. This is different than when someone's gender stays the same, but the words they use for it change. For example, if you talk with two people who went from identifying as young men to identifying as nonbinary, one might tell you they were always nonbinary and didn't have words for it, while the other might tell you they *were* a young man, until they weren't: their experience of their gender changed. Still other people experience their gender identity as continually shifting from day to day, and might describe themselves as gender-fluid.

> GENDER-FLUID: Describes someone whose gender identity (not only expression) might change from day to day.

The binary gender system teaches us to assume that biological sex and gender identity always line up in particular ways—for example, that everyone born with a vulva identifies as a woman, and no one born with a penis does. While it's true that most people born with a vulva grow up to identify as a woman, some grow up to identify as a man or as nonbinary, and of course the same is true of those born with a penis, and of intersex people born with genitals that are hard to categorize. When someone's gender identity does not line up with their body in the ways demanded by the binary gender system, they might be described as transgender (or trans)—meaning someone whose gender identity differs from what is expected of them in their culture and / or the dominant culture, and who usually has some sort of transition experience of going from living as one gender to living as another gender.

> TRANSGENDER (OR TRANS): Describes people whose gender identity differs from what is expected of them based on their sex assigned at birth.

> TRANSITION: Any and all of the personal, social, legal, physical, and sometimes spiritual processes that a person goes through in order to live their life as a gender that works for them.

Someone who is transgender can also be a man or a woman or genderqueer or another category. Compound gender identity labels like *trans man* and *trans woman* always refer to someone's current gender identity, so a trans woman is a woman who was assigned male at birth and raised as a boy for at least part of her childhood, while a trans man is a man who was assigned female at birth and raised as a girl for at least some of his childhood. Someone's current gender identity is often all you need to know about their gender; details of their assigned sex or how they might previously have identified and lived (including former names) are rarely relevant to everyday interactions. Terms like *trans man* and *trans woman*, which focus on someone's current identity, are generally considered more respectful and accurate than terms that emphasize body parts (such as biologically female, natal male, female-bodied, bio-male) or transition (like MtF, FtM).

Someone whose gender identity basically aligns with what's expected of them based on their assigned sex can be described as *cisgender*. Cisgender people can (and almost always do) also identify as a man or a woman. Cisgender men are people assigned male who live as men, and cisgender women are people assigned female who live as women. Cisgender is a relatively new word, and has been important and useful in giving us a way to talk about the specific experiences of men and women who are not trans, without simply defining cisgender people as what they're not. It has also given us ways to talk about the privileges experienced by people who are exempted from the specific forms of marginalization that trans people face for being trans.

> CISGENDER: Not trans.

Still, cisgender is an imperfect term. One critique of cisgender is that it sets up yet another binary: one is either trans or cis. Actually, gender experiences are sometimes more complicated than that. If you want to explore these ideas further, Finn Enke's essay "The Education of Little Cis" explores the emergence of cisgender as a concept, from both personal and academic perspectives, as well as some of the gray areas between cis and trans.

Trans is also used in a broader way, referring to anyone whose gender identity or *gender expression* differs from what's expected of them. This broad understanding of trans includes many people who would not necessarily identify as trans, such as masculine women and feminine men. That's pretty complicated, since it's generally not respectful to call someone a word they wouldn't call themself. On the other hand, the broad category of trans has been very useful as a social justice organizing tool, allowing us to talk about the whole range of people who are vulnerable to discrimination based on their gender identity or gender expression.

Since trans and transgender are used in so many different ways, it is really helpful when you use either term to clarify how broadly you mean it for the purpose of that conversation. Likewise when someone else speaks of trans people or transgender people, it's okay to ask which definition they're using.

Gender expression refers to behavior that communicates something about

GENDER EXPRESSION: Behavior that communicates something about gender, including clothes, mannerisms, etc.

gender, whether intentionally or unintentionally. It includes how you walk, how you talk, the words you use to describe yourself (including pronouns like he, she, they, ze and so on) and more. People sometimes describe gender expression as a binary of masculine and feminine, but of course masculinity and femininity are far from binary. There is a range of ways to be masculine and a range of ways to be feminine. Norms of masculinity and femininity are culturally specific and also can vary over time within a culture. What counts as feminine "enough" for, say, a woman in a professional office environment looks vastly different now than it did fifty years ago.

The binary gender system teaches us to assume that gender expression lines up with gender identity, or should—that all women are (or should be) feminine and all men are (or should be) masculine. Of course, that's not always true. Some women express themselves primarily through masculinity, and might describe themselves as masculine women or as butch, macha, AG, stud, or a variety of other terms. These women's gender expression doesn't necessarily make them not women—woman is a gender identity, and masculine is a gender expression. And, it's not always that straightforward—for some butch women, butch is about identity as well as expression, and is as much a part of their gender identity as woman. Some other women express themselves through a specifically queer femininity that differs from mainstream expectations of femininity, and might describe themselves as femme. Likewise, some men express themselves primarily through femininity, and might describe themselves as femme, queen, fey, and other terms. Some people use the term gender-nonconforming to describe folks whose gender expression differs from what's usually expected for people of their gender.

GENDER-NONCONFORMING: Describes people whose gender expression differs from what's usually expected for people of their gender.

Many of the terms for specific kinds of gender-nonconformity emerge from LGB and queer communities. Gender expression and sexual orientation relate to each other in complex ways, but they are not the same thing. Not every feminine man is gay; not every masculine woman is a lesbian. When we think we can guess someone's sexual orientation based solely on their gender expression, we will often guess wrong. People of any gender identity and expression—including any kind of trans identity—can have any sexual orientation.

QUEER: An umbrella term describing a wide range of people who do not conform to heterosexual and/or gender norms; and, a reclaimed derogatory slur taken as a political term to unite people who are marginalized because of their nonconformance to dominant gender identities and/or heterosexuality.

SEXUAL ORIENTATION: Someone's patterns of romantic and/or sexual attraction, in terms of the gender(s) of people they're attracted to.

Because gender expression is behavior, you can observe it—you can see how someone walks, observe how they talk, and so on. But you can very easily misinterpret what someone's gender expression means to them, especially across cultures. For example, in the dominant white U.S. culture, long hair on a man might be interpreted as part of a feminine gender expression, whereas in some Native American communities, long hair is an expected part of masculine expression.

On the other hand, gender identity is not observable. The only way you can know someone's gender identity is if they tell you.

Activity: Uncovering Gender Expression Assumptions

1. Think of a time when you made an assumption or a guess about someone, based on their observable gender expression. It might have been a guess about their sexual orientation, their interests, their skills, or something else.

2. On a piece of paper, draw a line down the middle to make two columns. In one column, write (or draw, if you like) what you actually observed about the person. In the other column, write down what you guessed about them. For example:

OBSERVED:	ASSUMED OR GUESSED:
· a large person · with pale, sunburned skin · wearing overalls and a baseball cap · stepped out of a pickup truck · in the library parking lot	· I assumed the person was a man. · I interpreted his demeanor as masculine. · I guessed he might do some kind of outdoor work, maybe carpentry (not office work). · I guessed he might be a the library to repair something there, rather than to get books.

Notice that the gender identity of the person, unless they actually told you, goes in the assumed or guessed column—because you can't observe gender identity!

3. Look at what you've written down and ask yourself, what would you have to believe about gender in general for your guesses about this person to make sense? For example, the last guess in the right column above only makes sense if you believe that people who are a certain kind of masculine don't read much.

4. Now ask yourself what else might be going on, in addition to gender. Is there something about race, class, culture, age, or something else that might have contributed to your assumptions or guesses? In the example above, assumptions about class, race and gender come together in stereotypes of "blue collar" labor.

5. Finally, what other, alternate story could you tell? If your initial assumptions and guesses were wrong, what might have been true instead?

If this book is your first introduction to these topics, this all might seem overwhelming. You might even feel more confused than you did before you started reading. That's okay! This stuff is far more complicated than how we're usually taught to think about it. Sometimes confusion is a really good sign that you are beginning to pay attention to the complexity of gender.

The key things to remember from this section are: biological sex, gender identity, and gender expression are different from each other. None of them are binary. All of them can change over time. And people can have any combination of them, because they are not necessarily attached to each other in the ways the binary gender system teaches us to expect.

This section has introduced a lot of terms that may be new to some readers. As noted in the introduction, the language we use to talk about gender and trans issues is constantly evolving. People use these terms in a variety of ways, and their usage has changed and will continue to change over time. When referring to an individual's identity, it's more important to understand what that person means by the terms they use, rather than to memorize the "standard" definitions.

Activity: Your Personal Genderbread Cookie

(This activity can be done solo, but is more fun with a friend.)

Although trans people often have to think through our genders in great detail, most cisgender people are never asked to describe their genders beyond a simple check box of M or F. But everyone's gender experience can be understood in a more nuanced way than that. For cisgender people, exploring your gender in all its nuances is one way to develop a foundation of self-awareness for your allyship.

Draw yourself a Genderbread Cookie like the one on p. 10. Where that cookie says "gender identity," write (or draw) your gender identity—what identity category or categories feels closest to your inner sense of yourself as a gendered person?

Where that cookie says "biological sex," write (or draw) about aspects of your physical body that are related to gender and/or reproduction, using whatever words and/or images work for you. Don't just write "male" or "female," get specific: What are your salient body parts or characteristics that are part of biological sex?

Where that cookie says "gender expression," write (or draw) yours: What do you do with your body, behavior, attire, and language that communicates something about gender (whether or not you mean it to)? Do people tend to understand your gender expression the same way you do? If not, what do they get wrong, and what do they tend to see instead?

Write or draw in anything else that feels relevant to you about your gender. Are there culturally-specific, class-specific, or race-specific experiences or understandings that are part of your gender? Is there something about your age or generational moment that places a particular twist on your gender? Is there something about

about your health or disabilities that affects your experience of your gender (or biological sex)? And anything else that feels important to include.

Finally, if you have been doing the activity with a friend: Share your genderbread cookies with each other. Talk through what you wrote/drew, what it makes you think and feel, and what you want each other to know about your genders.

CHAPTER THREE: *Trans Lives*

COMING OUT AND TRANSITION

Most trans people have some sort of transition experience—going from living their life as one gender (the one assigned at birth) to living their life as another gender. Transition looks different for everybody, and includes any and all of the personal, social, legal, physical and sometimes spiritual processes that a person goes through in order to live their life as a gender that works for them.

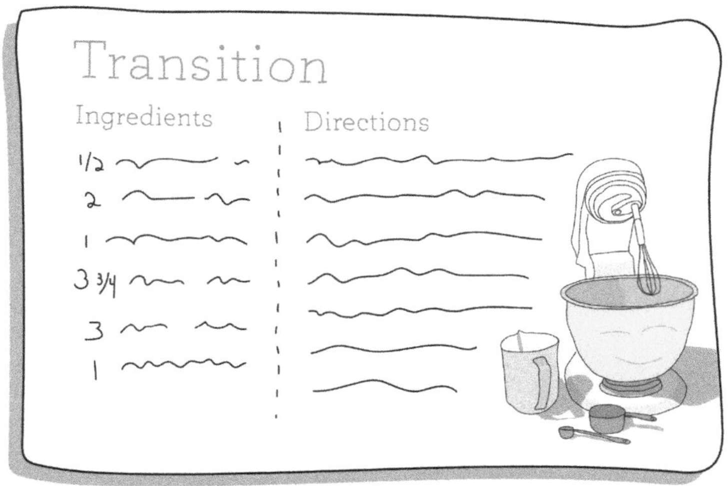

There is no right way to transition. People can use all, some or none of the options available to them. And people often don't have access to all of the options they want and need. People make a million complicated decisions about how to transition. There is no magic ingredient that makes a transition "complete."

Some trans people reach a point where they feel their transition is over, and they are "fully transitioned" and no longer transition*ing*. For others, transition is a lifelong process of exploration and adjustment. For some trans people, a gender transition is something they have to get out of the way in order to continue exploring other aspects of themselves; for others, it's not so separate, and continuing to explore gender is part of continuing to grow as a person. No one else gets to decide when someone's transition is "complete," and respecting someone's gender shouldn't depend on how complete their transition seems to you *or* to them.

Ingredients of Transition—Mix and Match!

PERSONAL

- Contemplating your gender and what it means to you
- Noticing feelings you might have been ignoring
- Contemplating what gender categories and labels "feel right"
- Contemplating what it would mean to live publicly as a different gender than you've been seen as up until now

SOCIAL

- Asking people to call you a different name
- Asking people to call you a different pronoun (he, she, they, ze, etc.)
- Some relationships shift as dynamics get re-negotiated, for example shifting from being an uncle to aunt, or a girlfriend to a genderqueer sweetie, or a woman friend to a man friend
- Changing your clothes and hair to styles that feel more aligned with your identity and/or how you want to be seen

LEGAL/CLERICAL

- Obtaining a court-ordered legal name change
- Obtaining a court-ordered change of gender
- Changing the name and gender category on id documents (driver's license, passport, etc.)
- Updating *everything* that has your name on it—bank accounts, school records, insurance, voting records, library card, gym membership, the label on your cubby, those cute return address labels from that one time you donated to the World Wildlife Fund...

PHYSICAL/MEDICAL

- Hormones
- Surgeries
- Exercise programs aimed at reshaping the body in gendered ways
- Tattoos, piercings, and other non-medical body modifications

SPIRITUAL/RELIGIOUS

- Name change ceremonies
- Coming of age rituals, e.g., an adult bar mitzvah for a trans man who may have already had a bat mitzvah as a girl

Reflection: Transitions

Not long ago, when visiting my home town, I found myself taking a walk with someone I hadn't seen in over 15 years. The last time she had seen me, I had been a teenage girl with very long hair, clumsy social skills, and an embarrassing lack of fashion sense. Now I had a little goatee, wore basic casual "guy" clothes that more or less matched, and held myself like a confident professional. "You're like a whole 'nother person," she said. "I'll have to get to know you all over again." She meant because of my gender. I thought, well of course I'm a whole 'nother person. It's been 15 years. I'm a grownup now, for one thing. She's probably a whole 'nother person, too.

In some ways, gender transitions are unique. But in other ways, they're much like any other major life transition. What have been the transitions in your life, whether gender-related or not, that make you feel or seem like "a whole 'nother person"? And how are you, at the same time, the same person as you always were?

"Coming out," in this context, simply means disclosing that you're trans. Like "coming out" around sexual orientation, coming out about gender is usually not a one-time announcement. For some people, their trans identity is private, and coming out is a rare event. Others might come out a dozen times a day. Coming out is not inherently healthy or unhealthy. People decide to be out or not in different contexts for many reasons including to protect their safety. No one should be pressured to come out or not come out.

For some trans people, strangers tend to assume they're a gender that they're not, or tend to guess right away that they're trans. In this situation, coming out means giving people information about the gender they are. Often this happens after someone makes an inaccurate assumption. If someone says, "Excuse me sir, can you help me find the Third Street bus stop?," coming out can be saying, "Actually I'm a woman, and it's just past that big brick building over there."

For other trans people, strangers usually or always assume they're the gender they are, and do not necessarily assume they are trans or that they used to live as another gender. For trans people in this situation, coming out means complicating people's understanding of their gender. It might sound like telling a colleague, "You know me as a woman, and you might

not realize that I didn't always live as a woman." Or it might sound like just letting something slip, like a trans man saying, "I love Girl Scout cookie season, too! When I was a Girl Scout...."

Because of the widespread discomfort and misunderstanding around trans identities, this kind of coming out can ironically lead people to understand a trans person's identity *less* clearly than they did before. For example, if someone is not very familiar with trans identities, knowing that someone is not only a woman but also a trans woman can lead them to doubt her authenticity as a woman. Sometimes people start to have trouble calling

A NOTE ABOUT "PASSING": "Passing" means being seen as belonging unquestionably to a particular group, e.g. being seen as a woman or as a man. Often, it refers to a trans person being seen as the gender they are; occasionally it refers to being seen as the gender that one wants to be seen as at the moment, for safety or other reasons. Some people use "passing" specifically to mean being seen as cisgender (e.g. a trans woman who is assumed by others to be a cisgender woman is "passing"), while for others it is not that specific. Passing is a very complex and problematic concept, not only with regard to trans issues but also in terms of race, class, and other systems of categorization and power.

someone the right pronouns (she, they, he, etc.) after finding out the person is trans, even though they were getting it right before. If that ever comes up for you, Chapter 4, "Getting Pronouns Right and What It Teaches Us About Gender," may be helpful.

Coming out as nonbinary is complicated in yet another way. Since the dominant culture doesn't have a way of understanding nonbinary identity, strangers almost always guess wrong about our genders. When we decide to tell them our identities, they may not recognize the words we use. Coming out as nonbinary often means educating the people around us about nonbinary identities, trans identities more generally, and our particular experiences. It is a huge amount of work, and can be emotionally costly especially when people are not receptive. Many people with nonbinary identities choose not to come out in some contexts, just to make it easier to navigate a social environment that doesn't quite have a place for us.

INTERSECTIONALITY

Wrapping your mind around the concepts and terminology used to talk about trans identities is important, but of course trans people's lives are more than our genders. For one thing, trans people are not only trans, but also all of our other identities at the same time. They all matter, and they all complicate each other. Legal scholar Kimberle Crenshaw first coined the term intersectionality to talk about how racism and sexism interact to create specific impacts on Black women that are more complicated than just the sum of racism as experienced by Black men and sexism as experienced by white women. Since then, other scholars and activists have further developed the concept to talk about how all kinds of identities are entangled with each other, as well as how systems like racism, sexism, classism, ableism, and so on are entangled and reinforce each other.

Intersectionality reminds us that the experience of being, for example, a trans woman who is Latina, cannot be understood simply as experiencing everything typical of trans women across races plus everything typical of Latinas whether trans or not—even if such generalizations could be made. Being Latina (and all the specificity of what kind of Latina, including stuff like nationality, immigration status, first language, etc.) impacts what it may mean for someone to experience herself as a trans woman, and being a trans woman impacts how she might understand her Latina-ness. Translatina emerges as its own thing—a very specific position from which someone experiences herself and the world, not as simple as the sum of trans and woman and Latina.

These intersections of identity affect the kinds of barriers trans people are likely to face in the world in some ways that are subtle, and other ways that are horribly blatant. For example, many white trans men (as well as transmasculine people who do not identify as men) have written about their experiences of gaining privilege when they started being perceived as men. (I get much better customer service in hardware stores when I'm perceived as a man, even a small and feminine man, than when I'm perceived as a woman.) But for trans men who are Black and/or Latino, being perceived as a man can make them vulnerable to unfriendly attention from police and security guards, differently than when they were perceived as women. They may also gain privilege in some contexts, but the two don't cancel each other out.

> TRANSMASCULINE (ADJ.): Usually used to describe trans people who are assigned female at birth and whose identity is more toward man than woman, including transgender men as well as some people with nonbinary gender identities. The term is imperfect in many ways—see the Glossary for a deeper explanation of its uses and complications.

Reflection: Intersectionality

How are your other identities intertwined with your gender? (You don't have to be trans to do this activity! Cisgender people have genders, too.) Consider identities like race, ethnicity, sexual orientation, disability, age/generation, religious/spiritual background, class background, culture, etc. How do they affect your understanding and experience of your gender? How does your gender affect your understanding and experience of your other identities?

How do systems of oppression impact how you experience your gender in the world? Consider not only sexism and cissexism (oppression of trans people) but also racism, classism, ableism, and so on.

And of course, beyond identities like race, class, disability, and so on, trans people also understand ourselves through all of our other interests and roles. If you are new to thinking about trans issues, when you meet a trans person, their being trans might seem like the most interesting thing about them. But to them, it might not be the most interesting thing. Maybe your trans neighbor or colleague or student is more interested in their role as an artist, scientist, caregiver or family member than they are in their gender identity.

TRANS CHILDREN AND YOUTH

People begin to articulate a transgender identity at a variety of ages—some in childhood, some as adolescents, and others as adults. Among those who come out as adults, many—but not all—say that they knew as young children and weren't able to express it.

Not every kid whose gender stands out as unusual is trans. Almost all young children engage in gender play, which can include cross dressing, taking on different gender roles in pretend play, and asking to be called a name that is not usually associated with the kid's assigned gender. Gender play is also common among teens in environments where it is accepted. Beyond play, some kids may have gender expression that's consistently different from what adults expect of them—masculine boys, feminine girls, and so on.

It is not always immediately obvious to adults whether a particular child is trans, in the sense that they will need to transition, or gender-non-conforming, or engaging in gender play. Fortunately, it is not necessary to know. Rather than trying to figure out what a child *is*, parents, teachers and service providers can focus on what a child *needs*, and trust that the rest will become clear with time. In order to acknowledge the experiences of kids whose gender stands out, without boxing them in to any assumption about how they will eventually identify, people sometimes refer to such kids as gender-creative, gender-expansive, or gender-independent.

Some trans children and youth choose to go through a social transition. Social transition means participating in family, school and other activities in accordance with the child's gender identity, rather than the assigned gender. It includes introducing the child to peers and adults using a name, pronouns, etc. that are appropriate for the child's stated gender.

Support from family and schools is crucial for social transition. However, the support should always follow the child's lead. Since more children are transitioning in a relatively public way, some people have become concerned that parents, over-eager to be supportive, are pushing their kids into a gender transition that may not be necessary—"making" them trans, in other words. Let's clear this up: You can't "make" a kid trans, any more than you can make a trans kid cis. Gender identity at all ages is pretty resistant to outside pressure to change. And the reality of many parents pressuring their kids to *not* be trans is a far more widespread and dangerous pattern than the reverse.

Still, it is important to remember that not every gender-expansive kid will want or need to transition. For example, if a nine-year-old who has been raised as a girl announces out of the blue, "I'm not a girl, and I want to be called Joey instead of Jolene," the family should not rush to change Joey's legal name and buy a whole set of school clothes from the boys' department. Joey may eventually need that kind of transition, or may not. Joey may be a trans boy, or perhaps a gender-nonconforming girl or tomboy, or maybe Joey will have a nonbinary gender identity. Even if Joey is a trans boy, he might be a feminine boy who enjoys wearing girls' clothes some or all of the time. We don't know yet, and it doesn't necessarily matter. Adults can support Joey by respecting what Joey wants right now, asking open-ended, nonjudgmental questions about what that means to Joey, and seeking support for themselves to manage their own expectations and wishes for Joey's gender.

In terms of medical transition, no medical steps are necessary or available before puberty. As trans children approach puberty, some will consider puberty blocking medications, which delay puberty until the child and family can make decisions about further medical transition steps. These are com-

If you're a parent of a trans kid (who's still a kid), it's especially important to get support for yourself as you support your child. All kinds of reactions are common and normal for parents of trans kids and kids exploring their gender. We live in a strictly binary culture, and it can take time to understand and accept something new. Getting the support you need will enable you to support your child well. Your local PFLAG group or LGBTQ Center may have resources or support groups specifically for parents of trans kids, and there are lots of online resources including Gender Spectrum, PFLAG, and various social media groups. And make sure to check out the section for parents of trans kids on pp. 83–85.

pletely reversible. After age 16 (or sometimes a little before), some trans youth with supportive parents begin hormone therapies to induce pubertal changes consistent with their gender identity. These treatments are considered partially reversible. After age 18 (or in rare cases, 16) trans youth can consider surgical interventions.

Although many families with trans kids benefit from working with a gender therapist, a therapist's diagnosis is not required to confirm that a child is trans—the child's own articulation of their identity is enough. A therapist's role with a trans kid often includes supporting the child and family in making decisions about social transition, assisting the parents and school to respect the child's identity, and facilitating access to medical transition as appropriate.

Like with adults, it's important to remember that trans kids are more than their genders. Trans children and youth are, above all, children and youth. They are playful and serious, artists and jocks, valedictorians and class clowns. They test boundaries, throw tantrums, laugh at fart jokes, and dazzle us with their brilliance. Being trans is one important aspect of their identity and experience; it does not define them.

DISCRIMINATION, VIOLENCE, AND DISRESPECT

Trans people face daily hurdles ranging from verbal and physical violence, to the repeated indignity of stares and insults, to the challenge of navigating systems that aren't designed to account for people like us. The 2015 US Trans Survey, conducted by the National Transgender Political Coalition, surveyed over 27 thousand trans people and found:

- About 10% had experienced violence from a family member in reaction to their gender.
- Almost 20% left a faith community due to rejection of their gender.
- Only 11% had been able to change all their identity documents to reflect their gender, and of those who had shown an ID that didn't match their current gender, a third were harassed, assaulted, or denied services as a result.
- Almost a quarter had lost a job opportunity in the past year because of their gender.
- More than three quarters of those who were out or perceived as trans while in K–12 schools had experienced some form of mistreatment there, including physical and sexual violence, name calling, and being denied access to restrooms.
- More than half of those who interacted with police officers who recognized them as trans experienced some form of mistreatment, and police officers frequently assumed that trans people—especially trans women of color—were doing sex work when they weren't.

The rates of violence and discrimination are magnified when they intersect with racism, classism, ableism, ageism and so on. Trans people who have done sex work for income are even more likely to report experiencing violence from friends, strangers and the police than other trans people. Trans children face even greater barriers in accessing healthcare than trans adults, especially if their families are not supportive. Trans people of color and trans immigrants face particular barriers in obtaining safe and stable employment, and are especially susceptible to violence from police.

Sometimes discrimination and mistreatment are obvious: A landlord offers someone an apartment, and then changes their mind when they realize the new tenant is trans. A classmate verbally denies a trans woman's identity by saying something like, "everyone knows you're not a *real* woman," and deliberately calls her "him" to drive home the point. A stranger assaults a trans person because they know they can get away with it—trans people have good reason not to go to the police for help, and those who assault trans people are rarely apprehended, much less convicted.

Other times, there may be no ill intent, but the simple fact of systems set up on a binary assumption leads to exclusion of trans people. A homeless shelter intake worker turns a trans person away because they can't figure out whether to send the person to the men's shelter or the women's shelter. A school holds separate gym classes for boys and girls, and a nonbinary trans kid is assigned by default to the group that matches their sex assigned at birth. My health insurance company refuses to give me information about my own account over the phone, because they perceive my voice as female and therefore don't believe I'm me.

Part of being an ally to trans individuals is listening for and understanding what real or potential barriers are coming up in their lives, and figuring out what you can do to help diminish those barriers—on an individual level, on an organizational level, or as an activist working for broader change.

Sometimes, even before that, we need to make sure we are not being one of those barriers, even unintentionally. This means developing the capacity to notice and correct when we might say something that unintentionally discredits a trans person's identity, or worse yet places them in danger. The next section takes a deeper dive into the specific skill of making sure you can always call people the pronouns they want to be called, including when their pronoun changes. At the same time, it uses pronouns and mispronouning as a window into some of the ways in which we might internalize assumptions of the binary gender system.

> MISPRONOUNING: Calling someone the wrong pronoun, whether intentionally or unintentionally. For example, calling someone he when she wants to be referred to as she.

CHAPTER FOUR:
Getting Pronouns Right and What It Teaches Us About Gender

Pronouns. Why are pronouns so hard? What makes it so easy to slip up and call your trans friend by a pronoun they don't use anymore—maybe even a pronoun they haven't used since before you knew them?

I lost count long ago of the number of times a friend or colleague called me the wrong pronoun even though they knew better, and then when I reminded them they said, "It's hard. We're trying." Their defensive response was difficult for me to hear, because it seemed to imply that my transition was harder for them than it was for me, or that the pace of my transition should depend on their comfort. Still, there was some truth in it and eventually I started to believe them: it really is difficult (sometimes), and "trying harder" isn't necessarily effective. Instead of asking them to try harder, I got curious about what exactly was making it difficult—what was in the way of their doing this simple allyship behavior that they obviously wanted to do?

I decided to investigate what exactly makes pronouns so challenging. I interviewed dozens of people about what makes it hard for them, if/when it is hard, to get someone's pronouns right. Based on their responses and my own experiences, I developed exercises to help people get pronouns right, and started using the exercises in some of my trans inclusion workshops. Over the years, participants talked to me about their challenges and about what helped, and I incorporated their responses into my work with allies. This chapter brings that work together: A compilation of insights, explanations and exercises that can help you figure out what is getting in your way, and to get past it, so that your good intentions can translate into respectful action. Along the way, you might learn some things about your own beliefs and thought processes around gender.

Getting pronouns right is important, but of course it is only one small piece of what trans allyship requires. Even though you might need to put significant thought and effort into it at first, it's important to recognize that calling someone the right pronouns is a pretty low bar. But together with the other informed, accountable action you embark on, making sure that you can reliably get pronouns right will help you come across as the respectful, committed and caring person you are.

Not everyone who accidentally calls someone the wrong pronouns is doing so for the same reasons. Some of the reasons outlined here might not be true for you, while others might be spot on. It's your job to think it through and figure out which of the patterns described are relevant for you.

Likewise, some of the exercises will be exactly what you need, and some won't. If it seems helpful, do it. If not, then it might not be the one for you (at least not right now). Some of the exercises can be done alone, while some require other people's participation. Whether or not you are doing the exercises together, sharing and discussing this chapter (or the whole book) with a friend will probably make it even more useful than reading it alone.

WHAT ARE PRONOUNS?

Grammatically, pronouns are words that we use in place of nouns, to avoid repeating those nouns. In this case, we're talking about the third person singular pronouns: he, him, his, she, her, and hers. In Standard English (and many other languages, but not all), third person singular pronouns are always gendered.

Most people like to get called one set of pronouns and not others—for example, *he, his and him* but not *she, hers and her*. (This is true of cisgender people as well as trans people.) Some people don't like to be called either of the two most common sets of pronouns, and instead ask to be called *they/their/them* as singular pronouns, or another set of "gender-neutral" or nonbinary pronouns, such as *ze/hirs/hir* (see the table on the following page for more details on some of the more commonly used pronouns). Other people don't like to be called any pronouns at all, and just want to be referred to by name.

In general, people want to be called the pronouns that "go with" their gender identity. However, sometimes a person might need to be called a pronoun that *doesn't* feel right to them, in order to preserve their safety and/or privacy. Or, a person may ask to be called the pronoun that works best for them in some situations—such as among people who are safe and understanding—but not in other situations—such as in front of their boss

> A NOTE ABOUT PRONOUN "PREFERENCE": You may hear people talk about "preferred gender pronouns" (or PGPs). Many trans people object to this phrase because the word "preferred" implies that it is only preferable, not mandatory, to call someone by the pronoun they have asked for. In this book I use "the right pronoun" or "the pronoun someone wants to be called" rather than PGP.

<table>
<tr><th>SUBJECT</th><th>OBJECT</th><th>POSSESSIVE (adjective)</th><th>POSSESSIVE (subject)</th><th>REFLEXIVE</th></tr>
<tr><td>He</td><td>Him</td><td>His</td><td>His</td><td>Himself</td></tr>
<tr><td colspan="5">He likes us to call him when his order is ready. That one is his. He'll pick it up himself.</td></tr>
<tr><td>She</td><td>Her</td><td>Her</td><td>Hers</td><td>Herself</td></tr>
<tr><td colspan="5">She likes us to call her when her order is ready. That one is hers. She'll pick it up herself.</td></tr>
<tr><td>They</td><td>Them</td><td>Their</td><td>Theirs</td><td>Themself; Themselves</td></tr>
<tr><td colspan="5">Singular: They like us to call them when their order is ready. That one is theirs. They'll pick it up themself.
Plural: They both like us to call them when their orders are ready. Those two are theirs. They'll pick them up themselves.</td></tr>
<tr><td>Ze* (sounds like zee)</td><td>Hir or Zir (both rhyme with ear)</td><td>Hir(s) or Zirs</td><td>Hirs or Zirs</td><td>Hirself or Zirself</td></tr>
<tr><td colspan="5">Ze likes us to call hir when hir (or hirs) order is ready. That one is hirs. Ze'll pick it up hirself. Or Ze likes us to call zir when zirs order is ready. That one is zirs. Ze'll pick it up zirself.</td></tr>
<tr><td>Ey (rhymes with hay)</td><td>Em</td><td>Eir (sounds like air)</td><td>Eirs (sounds like airs)</td><td>Eirself</td></tr>
<tr><td colspan="5">Ey likes us to call em when eir order is ready. That one is eirs. Ey'll pick it up eirself.</td></tr>
<tr><td>Per**</td><td>Per</td><td>Per</td><td>Pers</td><td>Perself</td></tr>
<tr><td colspan="5">Per likes us to call per when per order is ready. That one is pers. Per'll pick it up perself.</td></tr>
<tr><td>[no pronouns]</td><td>[no pronouns]</td><td>[no pronouns]</td><td>[no pronouns]</td><td>[no pronouns]</td></tr>
<tr><td colspan="5">Jordan likes us to call Jordan when Jordan's order is ready. That one is Jordan's. Jordan'll pick it up Jordanself.</td></tr>
</table>

* also spelled zie, sie or xie.

** short for person; from Marge Piercy's 1974 novel *Woman on the Edge of Time*.

if the person is not out at work. Like with gender identity, the pronouns someone wants to be called may change one or more times over of the course of their life.

When somebody tells you what pronoun they want to be called, or that they want to be called a different pronoun than before, they will not necessarily tell you why. The reason may be complex, and besides, you don't really need to know. All you need to know is which pronouns they want you to use when referring to them. If your relationship is very close they may also want to talk with you about their gender journey in more detail, but you can safely expect to have that conversation far less often than the conversation about pronouns.

Some people whose gender identities are outside the binary ask to be referred to using "gender-neutral" or nonbinary pronouns. Some of the more commonly used nonbinary pronouns are they/them/theirs (singular) and ze/hir/hirs. Not everyone with a nonbinary identity wants to be called nonbinary pronouns. When someone does ask to be called a nonbinary pronoun, it's important to respect their request.

Although many people call them "gender-neutral pronouns," I tend to say nonbinary instead, for several reasons: First, the implications of asking people to call you these pronouns are anything but "neutral." On the contrary, going by nonbinary pronouns can make a strong statement about one's personal and/or political relationship to gender. Also, in most other contexts, "gender-neutral" means inclusive of all genders or not gender-specific. (For example, a gender-neutral restroom is one that anybody can use, regardless of gender.) I prefer not to confuse that definition by also using "gender-neutral" to refer to pronouns that are specifically nonbinary.

They/them/theirs is a bit of an exception. It is the most commonly used nonbinary pronoun, and it's also used as an actually neutral pronoun, referring to hypothetical people whose gender is unknown. They/them/theirs has been used as a neutral singular in this way for the entire history of modern English, and recently some official arbiters of "correct" English, such as the Associated Press's style guide, have finally acknowledged that it is acceptable even in formal writing. More history and musing about the use of singular they can be found in the last section of this chapter, "How Using They As a Singular Pronoun Can Change the World."

Some people use nonbinary pronouns, especially they/them/theirs, to refer to everybody, as a way of challenging the binary assumptions in our languages. This is sometimes problematic, because many people (including many trans people) feel disrespected when they are not called by the gendered pronouns that feel right to them—especially by someone who definitely knows what the right pronoun would be.

WHY PRONOUNS MATTER

Most of the time, most people are on autopilot about pronouns. They call all women she, her and hers, and all men he, him and his. But being on autopilot doesn't always work. Sometimes—especially, but not only, when talking about trans people—it can lead you to call someone a pronoun that isn't what they're usually called or what they want to be called. For many trans people, it is one of the most painful things you could possibly call them.

Why would it be so painful? When you use a gendered pronoun about someone, you are in effect announcing that person's gender. Most people feel attached to their gender as a core aspect of their identity. When you announce it incorrectly, it can imply that you don't recognize or "believe in" the person's gender identity.

Being mispronouned can have a particular impact on trans people because, whereas most cisgender people can comfortably assume that their gender is obvious and legitimate, trans people's genders are contested. Many trans people—especially those whose transitions are recent, or who often experience strangers guessing their genders wrong, or who identify outside of the two socially sanctioned gender categories—are accustomed to our genders being questioned, ignored or denied in almost every interaction.

Many trans people experience physical and emotional violence based on others' denial of or objection to their gender identities. Pronoun slipups, however unintentional, are connected to the broader reality of systemic violence against trans people. At best, they indicate that the speaker may have an unconscious bias toward understanding the world through the lens of the binary gender system. At worst, they can communicate hostile intentions and signal real danger.

The specific impact on a trans person when someone calls them the wrong pronoun varies depending on the context, on the support they have access to, and on their relationship with the person who messed up. Possible impacts include:

- Annoyance
- Confusion
- Feeling unrecognized or invisible
- Feeling unreal or not really present, distanced or dissociative

- Triggering internalized oppression, feeling not womanly or manly "enough"
- Feeling disrespected
- Feeing unsafe
- Being "outed" to observers who weren't aware of their trans status
- Losing relationships with observers who weren't aware of their trans status
- Being targeted for violence based on their trans status

In addition to the impact on the person who you mispronouned, there's also an impact on you and your ability to show up as your best self. When you're trying hard to get someone's pronouns right and continually making mistakes, you end up putting a lot of energy into pronouns that could be better spent another way. Instead of focusing on the things you both value about your relationship, you can get stuck in a frustrating and unproductive cycle of feeling nervous, saying the wrong thing, feeling bad about having said the wrong thing, and saying the wrong thing again.

It's normal to mispronoun someone once or twice when they first change their pronoun. But it's important to learn from your mistakes quickly, so that you can get out of that cycle and move on to the conversation you want to be having, with everyone feeling respected, seen and safe.

There are many ways to answer the question of why it is important to call people the pronouns they want to be called. In some ways, the most important reason is *your* reason—why does it matter *to you*? The exercises below can help you clarify and solidify your motivation to do the work you need to do to get pronouns right.

Reflection: Clarifying Motivation

Think of one trans person for whom you have difficulty using the right pronouns. Who is this person? What is your relationship to this person? In your own words, why is it important for you to get this person's pronoun right? What could be the consequences for you and them of continuing to get the pronoun wrong? Take some time to write down your thoughts about this. Put the paper in a place where you will see it at least once a day. Read it over from time to time. Even if you don't read it every day, simply noticing that it's there can serve as a gentle reminder.

Check In: Commitment

If it feels appropriate, talk to the person about why it's important to you that you get their pronoun right. Saying it aloud to the person who is most affected reinforces your own motivation, and also lets the person know that you are taking this seriously.

Only do this if you two are close, and if you have asked for and received permission to talk with this person about your learning process. You may want support and company in this journey, and that's valid—but seek it out elsewhere, because it is not this person's responsibility. Rather than assuming that they will be available to help you (and everyone else) understand their gender or navigate their transition, take responsibility for doing your own work to be the ally you want to be, and invite this person to participate in your process *if* they choose to.

BARRIERS TO GETTING PRONOUNS RIGHT, AND HOW TO OVERCOME THEM

"I'm just not used to it"

The most obvious reason it may be hard to get someone's pronoun right is simply because it's a change. Whether you've known someone for two weeks or twenty years, if you got used to calling them one pronoun (and/or name) and now they're using a different one, you might have to work to change the habit.

In this situation, you have a unique opportunity to be a really valuable ally by doing what you need to do to get the person's pronouns right. Most trans people lose at least a few friends during transition. Some of those friends mean well, but get so caught up in their own discomfort about the transition that they can't get past it to find ways to support their trans friend. By calling someone the right pronouns even though it's hard, you can show them that you are one friend who they won't have to lose.

You can also demonstrate that the image of them that you have in your head is an image of who they are now, not an image of them in the past or as you wish they would be. By using the right pronouns you can say, "I see you, I recognize you, I accept that you are who you say you are."

If habit is all that's getting in your way, there is good news: it just takes practice. The practice exercises below can help.

Gossip (not really)

Talk about the person when the person is not around, using the pronouns the person has asked you to use. You don't have to be talking about the person's gender, just make a point to include the person in your regular chit chat about your day. If you know the person in a confidential setting, try talking about the person to yourself in private, such as in the shower. Get used to thinking, saying and hearing the person's name paired with the right pronoun.

Toy Story

Give names to several common household objects in your home. For any object that has gendered associations for you, give it another gendered name. (For example, your mixing bowl might be Jack and your chopping knife might be Dolores.)

While you're going about your daily routine, tell stories about the objects using the pronouns appropriate to their names. Tell the stories aloud. Actually saying and hearing the pronouns is an important part of this learning process.

Once you've got that down (after at least a few days, or however long it takes for the objects' new genders to feel "natural"), switch pronouns but not names. Now the mixing bowl would still be Jack, but her pronoun would be "she." Once that feels natural, switch back. Switch back again. Add additional objects or try using nonbinary pronouns to make the game more challenging.

This practice can help to limber up your pronoun-switching muscles. Rather than relying on what "feels right" to you about another person's gender, you're training yourself to use the pronoun you've been told is right for them.

Pet Pronouns

If you have a pet—especially one that you frequently talk to or about—change its pronoun. (Your pet won't mind. I promise.) Also change the other gendered words you use to refer to the pet. Call it "good girl," rather than "good boy," for example. If you're practicing using a nonbinary pronoun, avoid "boy" and "girl" and call it "good kitty," or "good dog." Call your pet the new pronouns and other gendered words consistently, correcting yourself when you slip up. Keep this up until using the new pronoun feels "natural" and effortless, plus a few days extra. Then, if you want more practice, change the pronoun again.

On top of being a great way to practice your pronoun agility, this activity can lead to awesome teachable moments in the dog park: "Clifford! Come here, girl! She just loves the dog park, I bring her here almost every day."

Accountability

If it feels appropriate, make a plan with the person about how they can remind you if you mess up. For example, can they interrupt you in the middle of a sentence to correct you? Can they call you the wrong pronoun each time you call them the wrong pronoun?

The point is not to be punitive, but to agree on a way that you can get immediate feedback and not slip into old habits, and they can let you know when your incorrect pronoun use is impacting them. Like the Commitment exercise above, you should only do this if you are close, and if both people agree to do this process together.

Community

Do it together! If someone in your community is transitioning, don't be afraid to connect with other people in your community about what that means to all of you. Talk with other allies who are also trying to be respectful. Agree to remind each other when you slip up, so that it's not always the trans person's responsibility to do it. Consider getting together to discuss any issues that might get in your way, to go over some of the exercises in this booklet, or just to practice.

Calling someone a recently-coined nonbinary pronoun (or title, like Mx.—parallel to Ms. or Mr., sounds like *mix*) can be especially difficult at first, simply because it is a new word. But you can do it! It just takes practice. In addition to the exercises above, try this:

Nonbinary Journaling

If you already keep a journal, continue writing about whatever it is you usually write about, but use nonbinary pronouns (whichever set you're trying to learn)—for everybody. If you don't already keep a journal, set aside 15 minutes a day to write about something that happened to you that day, using only nonbinary pronouns. You'll be surprised how quickly they flow "naturally" in your writing. Then it just takes a little getting used to, to use them in speech.

Close To Home: For Partners, Family Members, and Close Friends

For the people who are closest to someone who transitions, getting pronouns right can be a particular challenge. If your parent, child, sibling, lover, partner, or best friend since childhood is transitioning and wants to be called a different pronoun, the closeness of your relationship can make their transition feel personal—as though it's about your identity as well as theirs.

In a sense, this is an illusion. It's not about you and there's nothing you can do or could ever have done to make it happen or not happen. In another way, it is about you, because their identities have something to do with your identities. For example, if your child was assigned male at birth, you may be used to thinking of yourself as the parent of a son. Now she's transitioning and wants to be called she. It might be hard for you not only because it's hard to think of her as a woman, but also because it's hard to think of yourself as the parent of a daughter.

If it's your partner who's transitioning, there may be an additional element about sexual orientation. You may be used to thinking of yourself not only as someone who is partnered with someone of a particular gender, but as someone who *would only ever* be partnered with someone of a particular gender. Learning that your partner is transitioning may call into question your understanding of your own sexual orientation.

If any part of this sounds like it reflects something that's going on for you, try the following exercises.

Check In: Relational Identities

Check in with your loved one who's transitioning about relational identity words. For some trans people, it's true that transitioning means a shift in all the relational identities that might apply to them—wife, brother, father, aunt and so on. For others, it can feel okay or even great to live with the seeming-contradiction of, for example, being a guy who's always called he/him/his and is also someone's sister or daughter or mom. When someone transitions, their relational identities may change a lot, or they may not change at all. Rather than assuming, ask what they're thinking about that.

Reflection: Relational Identities

Journal and reflect on your own relational identities—as the father of a son, or as a wife who has a husband, or whatever it is—and on your sexual orientation if relevant (more on that below). Which of your identities feel implicated in the transition? How do you feel about that? What would it mean for you to shift your understanding of those identities? What would it mean for you not to shift your understanding of those identities?

This is your part of your loved one's transition. You may need space and time to figure out what it means to you. Creating opportunities for your own process will help you be grounded and realistic through the transition process and make you a far stronger ally in the end. In addition to reflecting individually, it can be helpful to talk with other people who have a similar relationship to a loved one who is trans.

Reflection: Sexual Orientation

Here are some questions to consider if your sexual orientation is in the mix: Does it feel like a *problem* for you to think of yourself as, for example, a lesbian whose partner is now a man, or a straight woman whose partner is genderqueer? Does it feel like a *contradiction* that's *not* a problem? Or does it only sound like a contradiction relative to the dominant understandings of sexual orientation, while in fact it makes perfect sense for you? Or something else? If it is a contradiction, how would it feel to sit with the contradiction? How would it feel to resolve the contradiction by thinking of your sexual orientation in a different way? You may not have answers immediately—that's okay! It's helpful to ask yourself these questions with open curiosity, rather than assuming that your partner's transition either *must* mean something or *can't* mean anything about your sexual orientation. Your partner's gender is what it is and is not negotiable, but *you* are the one who gets to decide what it means to you.

Pronouns and the Binary Gender System

As a reminder, the binary gender system refers to the faulty assumption that an individual's sex, gender identity, and gender expression always line up in predictable ways—for example, that everyone who is born with a uterus identifies as a woman and expresses herself through femininity—and further that there are two and only two sexes, and two and only two genders (where identity and expression are conflated). This is just

not true. At the same time, since most of us are taught to believe in this model, its impact on our lives is very real.

When you find yourself thinking "If only that person's body was more like what I usually think of as a female body, it would be easier to call the person 'she'," the gender binary system has snuck into your thinking. You're working on an assumption—even though you may not believe it consciously—that all women have bodies like those we usually call 'female,' and all men have bodies like those we usually call 'male'—or should. You're relying on the binary gender system, even though you know it's not an accurate reflection of human diversity. And this is heartbreaking because the binary gender system assumes and asserts that trans people don't exist. It especially asserts that nonbinary identified trans people don't exist. When you misgender someone based on your perception of their biology, you imply that trans people aren't real.

Sometimes the gender binary sneaks into people's thinking in a way that's not about bodies, but rather about gender roles—about womanly or manly behavior. For example, people have confided to me that it's hard for them to call a trans woman "she" if she walks "like a guy," communicates directly, or shows confidence in her viewpoints. People have told me it's hard to call me "he" because I'm "nice," good with kids, and artistic. In this case, it seems to me that the underlying assumption is not only that body type dictates gender, but also that gender dictates personality. Anyone whose mannerisms don't match the cultural expectations of womanly behavior, for example, doesn't really count as a woman.

Assumptions that link a gender group with a universal human trait, like having feelings, are not only oppressive to trans people; they are also sexism. They reinforce an expectation that women (including both trans and cisgender women) must be ladylike and men (including both trans and cisgender men) must be manly, or face the consequences—such as invisibility, exclusion, and violence. They can put pressure on trans and cisgender women and men to perform stereotypical versions of masculine or feminine gender expression, and can limit our expression and even imagination of who and how we might be. They erase and marginalize genderqueer and other nonbinary identified people. These assumptions are incredibly damaging to all of us. Rooting them out of our language and pronoun use goes hand in hand with rooting them out of other aspects of our thinking.

Pronouns and Medical Transition

Assumptions about gender can also sneak into our thinking and behavior in some specific ways related to medical transition. Most straightforwardly, people often find it easier to call someone the right pronouns after they've started to take hormones or after they've had transition-related surgery. This pattern implies an assumption that someone can be a woman if she *had* a body like those we usually categorize as male, but not if she *still* has such a body. This is problematic for a bunch of reasons:

- Trans people are the genders they know themselves to be, whether or not they choose to change their bodies (and whether or not they have access to acceptable choices).
- The assumption creates external pressure on trans people to change their bodies whether or not that's what they need for themselves.
- Medical transition can be costly; many trans people who want and need to utilize medical transition options are not able to

It's been easier to think of River as "they" since I questioned my assumptions about binary gender.

It's been easier to call Kyle "she" since I talked with her friend Beau about how he got used to calling her "she" after her transition.

It's been easier to call Noah "he" since I heard his teacher calling him "he" in class.

It's been easier to call Marco "they" since they shared with me why it's important to them.

Ever since I got better at calling Dallas "she," I notice myself questioning sexist gender norms about women in construction.

access them. Many health insurance policies specifically exclude transition-related care, even for the same medications and procedures they would cover for other reasons.

- It still buys into the sex/gender binary, by assuming that a man's body means a body that looks like those we usually categorize as male (whether it developed that way with or without medical intervention), and a woman's body means a body that looks like those we usually categorize as female (whether it developed that way with or without medical intervention). That's a tiny step further than implying that trans folks don't exist at all, but only a very tiny one.

Some people find it easier to call someone the right pronoun after the person has *announced plans* to take medical transition steps, even before their bodies start to change. When I decided I was going to start taking testosterone and started telling people that, several colleagues who had struggled with my pronouns suddenly found they were able to call me "he" with no problem. During the six months between deciding to take testosterone and actually getting a prescription, my body didn't change, and my identity didn't change, but people's belief in my gender did.

The underlying assumption that seemed to be playing out wasn't as simple as that I had to have a masculine body to be a guy. It was that I had to have the intention to have a masculine body. This reflects a widely-held—*but wrong*—belief that trans people who change their bodies are "really" the genders they say they are, while trans people who don't or can't change their bodies are not as real or legitimate.

Reflection: The Binary Gender System

If you notice some underlying beliefs poking through in your behavior around pronouns, whether those assumptions are about bodies, gender roles, medical transition or something else, here are some questions to reflect on. Use them as writing prompts for reflective journaling, or as prompts for discussion with someone you trust.

- Drawing on the examples above, what are some assumptions about gender that you have found yourself thinking or acting on? (Try to generate a list, not just one example.) How have they come up? How do you feel about that?
- Other than making it hard to use the right pronouns for a trans person you know, what else in your life might also be affected by these same assumptions? For example, how might they affect your relationships with people who have the same gender identity as you? What about your relationships across gender? How might it affect your interactions with children? With your students, clients or coworkers? How might it affect how you think about yourself?
- When you think about it consciously, in what ways do you agree and disagree with these assumptions? What *do* you believe about gender? What would it look like to act on those beliefs?

Interpersonal Factors

There are lots of ways that our feelings about someone—whether conscious or unconscious—can come out in our behavior, including in our pronoun use. For example, one time when I had been out as trans and working in trans community for about five years, a colleague of mine transitioned and I had the hardest time calling her by her new pronouns. By that point, I had known *a lot* of people who had changed their pronouns, and it had never been hard for me before.

At first, I couldn't understand what made this transition so challenging for me. I reflected with the help of a trusted friend, and before long I figured out why I was struggling with my colleague's pronouns—I didn't like her. I disagreed with some of how she was doing her job, and we were not getting along. It had nothing to do with her gender. Even if it had, that would obviously not be an okay reason to call her the wrong pronouns.

As soon as I recognized what was going on, it stopped being a barrier to my using the right pronouns, and I was able to call her the pronouns that she wanted easily and consistently. As a result, my attention (and probably hers, too) was freed up to figure out what our conflict was actually about. Had I not tried to figure it out, and instead kept beating myself up every time I got her pronoun wrong, we might never have had that opportunity to address our real disagreements and become better colleagues to each other. Because I figured out what was going on *with me* that made it hard for me to call her the right pronouns, I was able to show up with all the compassion and skill that I usually bring to professional relationships.

It's my belief that you are not obligated to like everybody, but you are obligated to treat everybody with basic respect and dignity, and that includes respecting their gender. If you have an issue with someone, take the opportunity to figure out what the issue is and decide what to do about it, rather than taking it out on their gender. Here are some more complicated examples of social or interpersonal factors that might get in the way of someone using the right pronouns....

Being in the Same Club

Sometimes, the pronoun you tend to default to for someone else depends on whether or not you perceive the other person as part of your in-group in terms of gender and/or sexual orientation. One person told me that she has seen many friends transition, and usually finds it easy to switch to

calling someone a new pronoun. But she described one time when it was harder. She is a queer and genderqueer woman, and for years her friend also identified that way. Their similarity in terms of gender was part of their relationship. When her friend's gender experience shifted and he started asking people to call him he/him/his, she struggled because she was used to seeing their genders as the same. She thought, "If he's a guy … what does that mean about me?" Of course, she knew that it didn't need to mean anything about her. But her feeling that her friend was "like her" made it difficult for her to separate his gender from her own. Maybe she even felt a little bit betrayed that he was moving away from an identity they had shared.

A similar dynamic can play out if you *don't* see someone as "in the club." If, as a cisgender woman, you meet a trans woman who, for whatever reason, you don't want to think of as "one of the girls," it may be harder to respect her gender pronouns than if you felt excited to welcome her into your circle. Sometimes the reason that you don't want to think of a trans person as part of your gender group might come from the same kind of implicit disbelief in trans identities that I described above as part of the binary gender system. Other times it might be about other differences, such as dif-

Reflection: In-Groups

What does it mean for you to see someone as "like" you or "not like" you in terms of gender? What does it mean for you to see someone as "like" or "not like" the kind of people you could be attracted to? How might that get in the way of your respecting their genders?

Reflections: Exploring Interpersonal Factors

This works best if you have one specific person in mind, for whom you have particular difficulty using the right pronouns. Through reflective journaling or discussion with someone you trust, explore the following questions:

- How do you feel about this person? Personally? Professionally? Politically?
- Who else in your life does this person remind you of? How do you feel about those people?
- How has your relationship with this person been positive? How has it been negative?
- If you were to describe this person to a good friend on another continent (who would never meet them, so you wouldn't feel bad about gossiping), what would you say?
- Do you find the person attractive? If so, how do you see this as aligning, or not, with your sexual orientation?
- If relevant, say aloud to yourself, "[The person's name] is like me. [The person's name] is one of us [or 'one of the guys/girls/however you describe yourself and your gender peers]." Notice how you feel when you say it. Do you want this person in your in-group? Why or why not?
- In one relatively short sentence, describe your feelings about this person and then add "and at the same time I respect (his/her/their/etc.) gender and can demonstrate my respect in my language when I refer to (him/her/them/

> etc.)"—using the pronoun the person has asked you to use, of course! Write it down, and put it somewhere that you'll see it every day. Say it aloud whenever you see it, until it feels true and the pronouns become a habit.

ferent race and class experiences, different styles of expressing femininity or masculinity, or different modes of interacting in same-gender spaces. In any case, if someone's discomfort about a perceived difference leads you to resist thinking of someone as part of your gender "club," using the wrong pronoun can be a conscious or unconscious way to reinforce that separation.

Sometimes it's not so much about being in the same gender club, as about being in the same dating pool. A trans woman I spoke with described how heterosexual cisgender men who find her attractive never seem to have any problem calling her "she," although they know she's trans. On the other hand, heterosexual men who accidentally call her "he" are never those who find her attractive—or at least they never admit to it. Perhaps the men who easily call her the right pronouns use their attraction to her as evidence that she's "really" a woman (which would be an interesting kind of sexism!). Or maybe it's that men who don't want to think that they could be attracted to a trans woman call her "he" as a sort of defense against finding her attractive—as a way to define her as outside the group of women they could possibly be attracted to.

Walls Have Ears

Are there some situations in which you consistently use the right pronouns for a trans friend, and other situations in which you tend to mess up? What does it depend on?

You might find that it depends on who else is in the room: the person you're talking about, other friends, colleagues, strangers, or no one. The difference is usually unconscious. In some cases, it may simply be that when the person you're talking about is not present it's easier to forget—especially if their pronoun change is recent. Even though that person can't hear you, it is still important to get their pronoun right. Other people may take your language as a cue about what is acceptable. If you say the wrong pronoun and don't correct yourself aloud, they may assume that it is okay for them to use the wrong pronoun as well.

Sometimes, the unconscious difference in pronoun use in different situations might be serving to help you avoid some kind of discomfort. If your

pronoun use tends to vary depending on who's listening, consider what discomfort you might be avoiding—even without intending to. For example, are you avoiding the discomfort of having to explain yourself to someone less familiar with trans issues than you are? Or the discomfort of worrying that you might be seen as weird for being close with trans people? Whatever it is, challenge yourself to make decisions with everyone's wellbeing in mind, rather than reacting instinctively to avoid discomfort.

Keep in mind that you can "out" someone, and potentially put them in danger, by using the wrong pronoun *or sometimes by using the right pronoun*. When someone has recently started using a new pronoun, it is a good practice to ask them who they've shared that information with already, and whether they want you to call them the new pronoun in all situations (thereby possibly outing them to some new people), or not. In some cases, they may ask you to wait until they've had a chance to spread the word themselves, or they may ask you to keep their transition confidential indefinitely. Deciding not to be out to everyone is a totally valid decision and does not make someone less trans.

Getting it Wrong

Sometimes you will get someone's pronouns wrong. How you respond to your slips is just as important as your efforts to get it right in the first place. When you realize you've made a mistake, you may feel confused or ashamed, and you may feel tempted to move on as if it never happened. On the other hand, you may be inclined to stop everything, apologize profusely, and explain at length how you are not the kind of person who normally messes up this kind of thing.

Either extreme can be harmful. Ignoring the slip-up lets the wrong pronoun sit in the room. It can draw attention to the person's gender and potentially out them to people in the room who didn't know. And it gives the impression that you don't notice or care that you misgendered someone. On the other extreme, making a big deal out of your mistake can also draw attention to the person's gender. It also makes the interaction about you and your feelings, and puts pressure on the trans person to comfort you about your mistake.

Instead, aim for something in the middle, with four simple steps:

1. Apologize.
2. Correct yourself (repeat what you said, but with the right pronoun).
3. Move on—continue the conversation where you left off.
4. Later, figure out what you need to do to avoid making the same mistake in the future.

For example, this might sound like, "Well he was saying earlier..."

"It's she."

"Oh, I'm sorry. *She* was saying earlier that a student in her morning class asked a really good question."

Another way to think of it is, when someone corrects you about their pronoun, consider it as if they have just told you that your fly is down. You wouldn't just keep talking as if they hadn't said anything, and you wouldn't go on and on about how you usually never make mistakes like that, or that the zipper is a little broken and just slips down sometimes, or that you didn't mean to offend. You'd acknowledge it. You'd fix it. And then you'd move on.

COMMUNITY NORMS ABOUT PRONOUNS

Some trans people (and most cisgender people) want their pronouns to be obvious. They assume that by expressing their gender in an obviously feminine way, for example, they are sending a clear signal that people should call them she/her/hers pronouns. And it's true that more often than not, an ally can make a good guess at someone's pronouns based on their gender expression.

Nevertheless, assuming that everyone's gender will be obvious is problematic, because not everyone's is. A feminine person does not necessarily identify as a woman and want to be called she/her/hers. A masculine person does not necessarily identify as a man and want to be called he/him/his. An androgynous-looking person, like anyone else, may identify as a man, woman, both, neither, and/or something else, and some people don't particularly identify with any of these categories. And masculine, feminine, and androgynous (along with other gender expression categories) are culturally-specific, time-bound, basically *made up* categories that mean different things to different people. The only *sure* way to know someone's gender identity (which you don't really need to know) and pronoun (which you often do need to know) is to ask them.

When we assume that people's genders are necessarily so obvious that we can guess, rather than ask, we put a great burden on people whose gender and/or culture varies from the dominant expectation. It becomes trans people's responsibility to present our genders convincingly. To be convincingly womanly, for example, means conforming to stereotyped and stylized versions of what it means to be a woman, which are unrealistic and restrictive to all women, trans and cisgender alike. Instead, we can make it everybody's responsibility to pay attention to how each person wants to be talked about. The practice of suspending assumptions and creating opportunities for people to describe their genders on their own terms—or to decline to describe them—resists sexism and cissexism and opens up the possibilities for everybody.

Different communities, schools and organizations have developed a variety of practices around pronouns aimed at taking the pressure off individual trans people and creating a gender-inclusive space for everyone. These practices also offer learning tools and support for folks who are new to learning about trans communities or are practicing being able to use everyone's pronouns correctly. None of these practices are perfect, and different options work best for different groups. Here are a few examples:

Toolbox: Community Pronoun Practices

NAME TAGS & JEWELRY

At some conferences and events, people are invited to print their pronouns on their name tags, or to use interchangeable pronoun ribbons that attach to the provided name badges. Similarly, some trans artists have begun producing pronoun buttons, pendants and other jewelry with pronouns on them that can be worn any time.

Pros: They set a norm that pronouns are not obvious (you can't "tell by looking" what someone wants to be called). They take the pressure off of people to share their pronouns and to ask other people about their pronouns. You don't have to worry about forgetting, because it's always right in front of you. And if someone gets your pronoun wrong, you can point to the name tag when you remind/correct them.

Cons: If it feels mandatory, it can put some trans people in awkward situations. People who use different pronouns in different contexts, who are not "out" in every area of their life, and/or who are in a process of exploring their gender and not sure what they want to be called, have no subtle way to opt out of sharing. It only works if everyone is committed to checking the name tags and then calling people what they want to be called. And of course, it doesn't work for people who have limited vision or literacy (including young children who don't read yet).

Even better: This practice works much better if supported by some community education, such as signs, handouts or announcements explaining why it's happening and how people should use it. In particular, make sure to explain that it is optional, and specify what should happen if someone chooses not to put a pronoun on their name tag (that is, no one should call that person any pronouns).

EMAIL SIGNATURES

In some workplaces, all staff put their pronouns in their email signatures as a default. For example:

> Davey Shlasko
> Think Again Training
> I use he/him/his and they/them/theirs pronouns (either or mixed)
> THINK AGAIN

Pros: Similar to name tags, but it only works if you first meet the person by email rather than by phone or in person.

Cons: Similar to name tags, with some added awkwardness because of the power dynamics inherent in most work places. For example, if your boss wants to make pronouns in the email signature mandatory, you might feel too intimidated to question that plan even if it's going to cause difficulties for you. Also, it can be unnecessarily outing, especially for staff members who use nonbinary pronouns.

Even better: The greatest benefit to this practice is that it signals that the organization is thinking about trans inclusion, and that the particular staff member understands that pronouns are not always obvious. As an alternative, or as an option for staff members who don't want to disclose their pronoun in their email signature, you could insert a line in the signature that says something like, "Our organization is committed to respecting gender diversity. Feel free to ask our pronouns and tell us yours!"

ALWAYS ASK

In some communities and spaces there is a strong social norm of asking the name and pronoun of every new person you meet, individually, as soon as you meet them.

Pros: Establishes a norm that pronouns are not obvious. Puts the onus on everyone to ask and learn people's pronouns.

Cons: It's pretty awkward, especially for people unfamiliar with the practice who may have no idea what they're being asked. And it sometimes seems to imply that someone's gender, vis-à-vis their pronoun, is the most important thing you could know about them. Why not first ask something more relevant, like "What brings you here?"

Even better: Practice asking everyone their pronouns individually, but not as soon as you meet them. Instead, wait until you are going to have to use a pronoun about them. Then ask, and tell them why you're asking. For example, "I'd like to introduce you to my friend Anthony, because you're both passionate about fostering shelter cats. I want to make sure to introduce you correctly, so what pronouns do you like to be called—he, she, they, or something else? And, am I pronouncing your name right?"

GO-ROUNDS

In formal environments such as meetings and classes, the facilitator or teacher can start by asking everyone to introduce themselves by sharing their name and pronoun.

Pros: Similar to name tags and email signatures.

Cons: Similar to name tags and email signatures, with some added pressure from sharing aloud, and the limitation that it requires everyone to listen well and remember everyone else's pronoun—which is actually a pretty high expectation for hearing, attention and memory.

Even better: This practice works much better if supported by some explanation of why it is happening, and communicating an expectation that people call others the requested pronouns. In particular, explain that it is optional, and specify what should happen if someone chooses not to share a pronoun (that is, no one should call that person any pronouns). In ongoing groups that may build high enough levels of trust, you can also specify that people may use different pronouns in different spaces, and ask the group to commit to using the requested pronoun in this space, and asking before using any pronouns about each other in other spaces. You can make this practice more universally accessible by pairing with name tags, so that people have opportunities to both hear and see each other's pronouns.

INTAKE FORMS

In settings where one customer, client, or patient may interact with many staff members, an intake form can include a question about pronouns. Some teachers use a similar practice, asking each student to submit an index card on the first day of class indicating their name on the roster, the name they want to be called, the pronouns they want to be called, and anything else they want the teacher to know.

Pros: Demonstrates a commitment to trans inclusion. Gives a low-pressure way for people to share their pronoun.

Cons: Relies on all staff members to read, remember and use the right pronoun. In some cases, the intake form is too soon to ask, because the person hasn't yet had a chance to assess the friendliness of the organization/class and decide what pronoun to use there. In classrooms, the teacher is the only one who receives the information, so it isn't very helpful for discussion-based classes where students will need to know each other's pronouns.

Even better: This works best if all the record-keeping systems are aligned so that once a person writes a pronoun on an intake form, everyone who interacts with that person's records in any way will see the information. It's also helpful to provide another opportunity to state a pronoun, later on in the person's interaction with the organization (for example, in an intake conversation or in the second or third appointment).

SIGN-IN SHEET

In some youth groups, schools, and trans support groups, people are invited to sign in every day with the name they want to be called that day, the name they were called last time, and the pronouns they want to be called that day. Everyone knows to check the sign in sheet to see if anyone's name and/or pronoun has changed.

Pros: Allows gender-fluid people and people who are exploring their identity to request different names and pronouns on different days. Puts the responsibility on everyone to keep track of what people want to be called currently.

Cons: This only works if the group is committed to checking the sign-in sheet and using the names and pronouns everyone has requested.

All of the group practices around pronouns are far more effective when paired with information and support to help everyone understand the purpose and importance of sharing pronouns. When they're not contextualized with basic education, group pronoun disclosure can actually backfire, both by putting trans people on the spot and by provoking resistance or resentment from cisgender people who don't understand why they're being asked to change the way they speak.

Before you leap to introducing a new pronoun practice in your group, consider what additional context and resources would help the group implement the practice well. You might want to share this book or a shorter article, schedule a workshop, or show a video. Or, you might start by making connections between existing norms or values of the group and the practice of sharing pronouns. Your goal should be to get people to *want* to learn and use everyone's correct pronouns, rather than feeling forced to. It's not just about using the right words because they're right, it's about using the right words as a way to express respect and support to people who are part of the community and who we care about.

Activity: Group Practices for Pronouns

Are you part of a group that uses one of the practices above, or another like them, to encourage people to respect each other's pronouns? How is it going for the trans people in the group? How is it going for the cisgender people? If there's anything that's not working well about the practice, how could you improve upon it?

Are you part of a group that does *not* have any practices or norms in place to encourage people to respect each other's pronouns? Think about which of the above practices might work well for that group. If you know of trans people in the group, check in with them about how introducing one of these practices would feel to them. Consider introducing a group pronoun practice to the group, beginning with educating the group about why it's important.

HOW USING THEY AS A SINGULAR PRONOUN CAN CHANGE THE WORLD

A version of this section was first published on feministing.com in February 2015.

Some people who are otherwise committed to respecting trans people (and everyone) by calling them the right pronouns still struggle to use they as a singular pronoun. By now you know that it's both important and possible to call everyone the pronoun they want to be called, even if it's uncomfortable for you at first, as a way of showing basic respect for each other's identities. But there's even more to singular they than respecting individuals who use it. Singular they has exciting potential to be part of a radical shift in the dominant gender culture.

Changing the culture may seem like a mighty task for one little pronoun. But actually, it wouldn't be the first time that a pronoun was near the center of a momentous cultural shift.

One of the main excuses that people give for not using singular they, even when someone has specifically asked to be referred to that way, is that it is "grammatically incorrect." This belief comes less from a nuanced understanding of grammar than from a felt sense that you are doing something wrong by using singular they. As someone told me recently, "It sounds like nails on a chalk board."

Singular they may sound "wrong" at first because many of us were taught, corrected, and even disciplined in school to stop us from using they as a singular. Our teachers had to go to a lot of trouble to teach us this because otherwise, we would have used singular they all the time—because despite being frowned upon by so many middle school teachers, it is actually a totally normal thing to do in Standard English.

Since long before it started being adopted by trans communities, people have used singular they to refer to a hypothetical person whose gender is unknown. It's especially common in reference to a noun that is syntactically singular but logically plural, like "someone," "anyone," and "whoever." We say things like, "Someone left their umbrella in the meeting room." We *could* say, "Someone left his or her umbrella," but using "their" is more common, easier to understand and not wrong. Published examples of this usage abound, from as early as Chaucer through the present day.

The rule against using singular they is enforced neither because it preserves some consistent, objective grammatical standard, nor because it serves our communication needs. It is enforced because enforcing language norms is a way of enforcing power structures.

Practically everybody uses singular they in informal settings. I've even heard people use it unconsciously while explaining to me why they refuse to use it: "I don't use singular they even if someone asks me to, because I shouldn't have to change my grammar just to make *them* comfortable." Did you catch that?

The skill of avoiding singular they in formal settings is both a marker of privilege and provides access to further privilege. It's a marker of privilege because the grammar rule against singular they is part of Standard English,

which is "Standard" only because it is the dialect of the dominant, white, upper-middle/owning class culture, not because of an inherent superiority. People who grow up in the dominant community/culture learn to use Standard English, at least in formal settings, without even trying.

In schools, children who grow up speaking other varieties of English at home (as well as those who speak languages other than English at home) are disciplined to conform to Standard English norms. Depending on their relationship to schooling—how safe, welcoming and relevant they find it, for example—some kids learn to use Standard English in contexts where it's demanded. Others don't. The kids who don't internalize the rules of Standard English are not necessarily "failing" to do so. Sometimes, the "failure" to learn is actually successful resistance against an education system that is falsely telling them that they and their whole communities are bad and wrong for the way they speak. Even the kids who do learn to speak Standard English when needed usually continue speaking the way their families and communities do at home.

Following the rules of Standard English, including avoiding singular they, provides access to further privilege because those who do so in formal situations come across as proper and educated, and stand to benefit from being perceived that way. For example, they may have an easier time getting hired for a job or approved to rent an apartment. The rule functions to differentiate those who follow the rule from those who don't, those with greater privilege from those with less. In other words, it reproduces power differences. People who object to singular they on the basis of its being "incorrect" are not only dropping the ball on an important trans allyship behavior; they're also supporting a language/power system that harms millions of people across and beyond trans communities.

There's also another, more specific sense in which our pronoun problem is actually a power problem. It's not only the way the rule is enforced, but also how gendered pronouns work to begin with, that supports power structures.

People with nonbinary gender identities continually face situations in which someone feels "forced," by the Standard English norms they've internalized, to call us either he or she—even if they're not sure which one is right, and sometimes even if they have been told that neither is right. These moments, which seem to be about grammar rules, highlight a *gender* rule that doesn't work for us—the rule that everyone must be either a he or a she, a man or a woman—that there are no nonbinary genders. Avoiding singular they when talking about someone who has asked to be called "they" contributes to the erasure of nonbinary identities, and implicitly supports the physical, emotional and structural violence that faces too many of us too much of the time.

The good news is that singular they is not only coming into more common use, but also has the potential to help shift the harmful power structure of binary gender *and* of enforced, dominant culture language norms. To explain, it helps to go back to another time when what was considered standard usage for pronouns changed—and it had to do with power then, too.

Today, "you" is both a plural and a singular. Originally it was plural (the singular form was "thou/thee/thine"). Beginning in the 16th Century, "you" was also used for singular-formal address, when speaking to someone with high social status (royalty and nobility). Gradually, singular use of "you" expanded, first to any time a speaker addressed someone of higher status than themself, and then to any situation in which the speaker wanted to flatter or show respect for the person they were addressing. "Thou" gradually fell out of use until it was heard mostly in intimate settings, such as among family members, and in situations of obvious hierarchy, such as a wealthy employer speaking to their servant. To call a stranger "thou" became an insult, because it implied they were of lower status than the speaker.

The difference between "you" and "thou" was one of class status. The decision to say "you" or "thou" in a given situation had real consequences in terms of status and power. It could highlight and reproduce a status difference and power-over relationship, or it could downplay a status difference and create a tone of equality.

One driving force behind the drift from using "you" only for royal/noble address to using "you" for any respectful address was the relatively stable and powerful middle class in England at the time. Merchants and professionals increasingly saw themselves as entitled to respect of a kind that only the ruling class had previously been afforded. Using "you" with each other was a way to manifest that respect. Eventually, "you" became the only second person pronoun in general use.

As a result of this shift, the expression of class hierarchy in language became less mandatory. It became possible to construct a normal-sounding and easily understood sentence without knowing the status of the person you were addressing. The shift in language both resulted from and contributed to the shifting class structure.

We can use pronouns to shift the gender structure, too. Using singular they means we can construct a normal-sounding and easily understood sentence without knowing or announcing the gender of the person we're speaking about. We can talk about gender diversity in all its nonbinary complexity, without constantly contradicting ourselves by using binary gendered pronouns.

So please, make the effort to get comfortable using singular they. At least you'll be able to show respect to your nonbinary friends. At most, we might just change the world.

How Singular They Sounds

Chris brings their friend Tracy to a neighbor's house party. They enjoy meeting new people, but she mostly enjoys meeting the cats. Still, they both have a great time.

Chris always forgets something when they stay out late—this time, they forget their umbrella. Tracy never forgets things. She grabs the umbrella and texts Chris to let them know that she'll drop it off on their porch on her way to work tomorrow.

As you can see, singular they is usually used with plural verb forms (like "they forget," in contrast to "she forgets"). This means that you will use different verb forms about the same person, even in the same sentence, depending whether you're using their name or a pronoun (such as "Chris forgets" and "they forget"). This may sound confusing, but it will probably start to feel natural pretty quickly because it works just like "you." We say "you are" whether speaking to one person or many, not "you art" (as with the archaic singular, "thou art"). Likewise, we say "they are" whether talking about several people or one person, not "they is" (unless "they is" is part of your dialect anyway). However, most people say "themself" rather than "themselves" when referring to one person.

Just like with "you," we can use names and numerical adjectives (like "both," "all," and "one") to clarify whether we're using they as singular or plural. In the sentence, "They enjoy meeting new people, but she mostly enjoys meeting the house cats," the two pronouns—they and she—are both used singularly, and distinguish between the two people named earlier. Of course, that only works if the person you're speaking to knows Chris and Tracy and knows which pronouns they each use.

People often ask me about the "correct" way to use singular they, but the truth is, shifts in language don't happen all at once. You may hear people use singular they differently than outlined here, and only time will show which usage will become standardized as "correct." Focus on communicating successfully and respecting the preferences of the trans people and communities you are interacting with, and soon it will make as much sense as anything else about English grammar.

CHAPTER FIVE: *Allyship in Action*

Allyship is more than an attitude or identity. To move from being trans-"friendly" to doing effective allyship, you have to take action. This section outlines a few examples of concrete actions you can take to be an ally to individual trans people in your life.

In Chapter 1, "What is Allyship," I explain how one important facet of allyship is accountability—being in relationships that provide feedback and input to keep your allyship on track. While you're taking action, remember who you're accountable to. First and foremost, you are accountable to the person to whom you are trying to be a better ally. Beyond that, it's helpful to have relationships of accountability across the diverse spectrum of trans identities, so that you don't accidentally push one person down the hill while trying to help another person up.

Often, the first step you should take is to ask a trans person in your life what kind of allyship they want from you. But, since the dominant culture tends to discourage people from asking for help, it is useful to have a few specific offers in mind. This shows the person that you're serious about wanting to support them and have put some thought into what you're able to offer.

Here are some examples of allyship behaviors that are almost always helpful, and others that are sometimes helpful in particular circumstances. Some of the examples may seem incredibly obvious when you read them, and in some ways they should be obvious. But because of the way binary gender works, they are not always automatic. That makes it all the more important to incorporate these allyship behaviors into your life.

Remember, no single example from this list will make you some kind allyship superhero. Think of them as a tool box that, along with ongoing awareness, analysis and accountability, will help you continually build and hone your allyship skills.

EXAMPLES OF ALLYSHIP BEHAVIORS

Use Appropriate Language

It is always helpful to refer to trans people using accurate, up-to-date, and respectful terminology. Terminology is constantly evolving, and sometimes you will use a term that you don't realize has gone out of favor. That's not the end of the world. Just like with pronouns, you can apologize, correct yourself, and move on. And, recognize that it is your responsibility to pay attention to how trans communities refer to themselves and ask to be referred to, and to change your language to keep up with the times. If you're not sure whether a word is still standard to use, check the websites of trans-led advocacy groups, especially those connected to the particular local trans community you're talking about, to see what language they're using.

Remember that there is enormous diversity within trans communities, and words that some trans people are fine with may be offensive to others. For example, you may hear older trans folks using "transsexuals" to mean any trans people who transition medically, whereas most younger trans folks and trans-led advocacy organizations understand transsexual to mean a very specific kind of trans identity, and transgender to be a more respectful umbrella term. In some trans communities, particularly in communities where few people have access to higher education, you may hear people using "transgenders" as a noun, whereas many other trans people find that use objectifying and only use transgender as an adjective, as in "transgender people." Likewise, you may hear some trans people call themselves "transgendered," even though most trans advocacy organizations moved away from that decades ago (and Standard English eventually followed).

As an ally—including as an ally who's also trans—it's almost never appropriate to "correct" someone about the language they use for themself, even if it sounds incorrect or offensive to you. However, that doesn't mean you should describe them in the same way. When you're talking about particular trans people other than yourself, *ask* how they'd like to be referred to. When you're talking about trans people in general, use language like "trans people," "trans and gender-nonconforming people" (if that's what you mean), or "trans communities."

The language chart on pp. 68–69 is *not* comprehensive, but it is a good place to start in terms of recognizing which terms are most commonly used and understood as respectful, and which terms are often understood as offensive. Remember, language varies across different trans communities, and will continue evolving over time. Feel free to write in your own updates as you learn what language is being used in communities you interact with!

As in many marginalized communities, some labels that are generally offensive are also reclaimed as positive terms of self-identification by trans people. Remember that just because someone refers to themself with a reclaimed term, that does not mean it is okay for you to use the same word about that person or about trans people in general.

Appropriate vs. Inappropriate Language to Talk About Trans and Cis People

DON'T SAY...	BECAUSE...	INSTEAD, TRY SOMETHING LIKE...
Transgender*s*	Transgender is an adjective, not a noun. Referring to trans people as transgender*s* can sound dehumanizing.	Transgender people, trans people, trans folks
Transgender*ed*	Transgender is not a verb, so it doesn't need an –ed ending. Also, this makes it sound like being trans is something that happened to someone, like an injury, rather than an internal characteristic.	Transgender or trans
Transsexual	Transsexual is a word coined by medical professionals who were seeking to diagnose and ultimately "cure" transsexuals. The word carries some negative baggage from this history. Although some trans people still use it for themselves, many do not, and it's definitely not appropriate as an umbrella term for all trans people.	Transgender
Hermaphrodite	First, it's biologically inaccurate: although some animals can be "true hermaphrodites" in the sense of having two complete reproductive systems, humans cannot. Second, because the term originally referred to a mythological character, it can imply that intersex people are supernatural or imaginary. Finally, as a medical diagnosis that has been used to pathologize and mistreat people, it has a lot of negative baggage.	Intersex
Transvestite	Like transsexual, transvestite originated as a term of medical diagnosis. Many people diagnosed as transvestites were "treated" with coercive and abusive practices, and some were institutionalized. The term carries some negative baggage from this history.	Crossdresser
Tranny	Tranny seems to have originated both in the porn industry, as a trade name for porn involving trans women, and in trans communities (perhaps as a reclaimed term or perhaps independently). It also has been used as a violent slur, especially against trans	Trans woman or trans person

	women. For a while, it was common to hear trans women, trans men, and nonbinary trans folks use it as a reclaimed term. More recently, some people have pointed out that because different kinds of trans people are not equally targeted by it, it's not everyone's to reclaim. Now, most people consider it appropriate *only* as a reclaimed term for trans women who want to refer to themselves that way.	
He-she	This term originated in the porn industry as a trade name for porn involving trans women. It comes across as fetishizing and dehumanizing.	Trans woman
"Man in a dress"	Too often, this is used to mean a trans woman. That is inaccurate and disrespectful. If you see someone wearing a dress who appears to be male-assigned, you don't necessarily know how the person identifies.	"That's a nice dress you're wearing."
Bio-male, natal female, born male, bio-female, "born a boy," etc.	These terms emphasize body parts over identity, and imply that assigned sex category (male or female) is an accurate and complete representation of someone's sexed/gendered body (see pp. 11–12, 15).	Assigned male at birth (AMAB), male-assigned, or assigned female at birth (AFAB), female-assigned
Real woman, normal man, etc.	These ways of describing cisgender people imply that trans people aren't real, and therefore are super disrespectful to trans people.	Cisgender man or cisgender woman
Male-identified, female-identified	These terms are not the worst, but they sort of imply that someone only *identifies as* their gender rather than that they *are* their gender.	Male or man, female or woman
MtF (male-to-female) or FtM (female-to-male)	These terms emphasize body parts and transition history over current identity.	Trans woman, trans man

But it's just a word! … Right?

Sometimes it can feel frustrating if you are trying to be an ally, and someone criticizes you or distrusts your allyship because you've used a word they find disrespectful. It may be especially frustrating if you don't know why a term is considered disrespectful. If you're not following them closely, the evolutions in acceptable language about trans communities might even seem like arbitrary fads designed to keep you guessing.

For many of the terms that have come to be considered derogatory, the changes are anything but random. The terms have histories and origins that, once you understand them, make the negative implications clear. As these histories become known within trans communities, momentum builds to replace them with words that don't share that baggage.

The general principle at stake here is that individuals and communities deserve self-determination in how they are defined and described. When cisgender people (especially those with authoritative platforms, such as journalists or medical researchers) claim the power to name and define trans people, that harms trans communities. There are parallels here with other facets of identity, such as race and disability. In both cases, social movements over the past century or so have included pushes for shifts in language toward empowered self-definition, and away from definitions imposed by institutions and people with power.

If a trans person tells you that they feel hurt by a word you used, it is not that trans person's responsibility to educate you about why the word might be hurtful. But you can safely assume there is a reason, and a little bit of internet research can usually turn up all the background you could want. Even if you are unable to identify any particular logic in why a trans community asks to be called one word and not another, the fact that they are asking for it is a really important reason in itself. In the meanwhile, you can respond similarly to when you make a mistake with pronouns: apologize, correct yourself, and move on.

Use Current Names and Pronouns

Call trans people their current names and pronouns, always. If this is a challenge for you, review Chapter 4, "Getting Pronouns Right and What It Teaches Us About Gender," and do whatever practice and reflection you need in order to start doing this consistently.

Respect Privacy

Don't ask inappropriately personal questions of a trans person you've just met, such as "How do you have sex?" "What do your genitals look like?" or "How did your parents react to your transition?" If you have curiosity about a trans person's experience, ask yourself whether such a question is appropriate to the relationship you have with that person. And *always* give them an out: "I know this is personal, and you can totally feel free to say no, but I was wondering if you'd like to talk about your experience with ___ some time."

Don't Out People

Respecting trans people's privacy includes not disclosing their trans status unless they specifically ask you to disclose it. Maintaining some degree of control over how out we are, and to whom, is an important way trans people keep ourselves safe. Remember that using the wrong pronoun can out someone—and sometimes using the right pronoun can too, if the person isn't always perceived as their gender or if you're talking to someone who has known them by a previous name/pronoun. It can be helpful to ask in advance how someone wants to be referred to in front of people who may not be aware of their trans identity, and in particular settings such as at work or in front of their parents.

Treat People as Individual, Whole People

Remember that trans people are not only trans—we're also people! We have interests, identities, and experiences beyond and unrelated to our genders. If you want to be an ally to someone you don't yet know well, get to know them by taking an interest in aspects of their life besides their gender.

Treating someone as a whole person also means avoiding assumptions. Every person's story is unique. When you learn that someone is trans, you still don't know much about their particular journey, their feelings about their gender, their relationship to trans or LGBTQ communities, their sexual orientation, etc.

Educate Yourself

You've already taken a first step by picking up this book. But there's a lot more to learn. Take the initiative to look up books, articles, and organizations that can help you learn more about trans communities. I've offered suggestions throughout the book and in the resource section at the end. Depending on when you're reading this, the list may be out of date! I hope you will supplement it with your own current and local resources, especially those created by trans people. Don't wait until you mess up to go looking for updates or information—always assume you have something to learn. Build relationships with other trans allies to help motivate each other and hold each other accountable to your ongoing self-education.

Apologize

When you make a mistake—which you will, because we're all human—offer a real apology. Apologize without excuses, and without implicitly leaning on your trans friend to forgive or pardon you. Do what you can to repair the harm caused by your mistake, and do the work you need to do to avoid making a similar mistake in the future. In short: Apologize, correct yourself, and move on.

Bathrooms

Using public restrooms can be a particularly stressful and sometimes dan-

gerous experience for trans people who strangers often perceive as trans or as not their gender. Too often strangers feel free to question, harass and assault trans people for using the restroom that matches their gender identity, especially in the context of recent legislative efforts to restrict trans people from using the right restroom. This also applies to gender-nonconforming people who may not identify as trans.

If you're with a trans friend in a public place, you can often help simply by going to the restroom yourself, and then describing the layout to your friend. Knowing ahead of time whether the restrooms are single-stall, whether they're marked as gender-specific, whether there's a line, and whether the doors and locks are in working order can do a lot to alleviate the anxiety of walking into a public restroom. Many trans men don't use urinals, so with men's rooms it's also helpful to know how many stalls there are and whether they're all in use (even if there's no wait for the urinals).

If you use the same restroom as your friend, you can offer to go with them. Strangers will be far more reluctant to question someone who they see is not there alone. When you accompany your friend to the restroom, act as you normally would in a restroom. If you don't need the restroom yourself, wash your hands so that you don't look like you're loitering. (Actually, wash your hands no matter what.) If the two of you have identified that someone is likely to challenge your friend despite being with a buddy, talk in advance about what kind of response would feel most helpful. Be mindful that intervening in a way that escalates tension or results in security being called may do more harm than good.

Bathrooms are such an important site for trans allyship that campaigns and technologies have sprung up around helping trans people stay safe there. For example, #IllGoWithYou is a campaign of trans allies who offer to accompany trans folks who need a bathroom buddy. People wear #IllGoWithYou pins, stickers and key chains to show that they're available for that kind of support. Of course, most trans people don't usually want or need a stranger to accompany them to the restroom. But signaling that you *would* go with is still a way to show that you are a safe person and a potential ally-on-call. There are also a number of apps that map trans-friendly restrooms, such as Refuge Restrooms.

Correct Misgendering and Other Disrespectful Talk

One fantastic ally action is to respond when you hear people speaking disrespectfully about a trans person or about trans people in general. For example:

- In the break room at work, you hear Michelle call Lara "he," but you know that Lara has asked all your coworkers to call her "she." You can gently correct Michelle, "I think you meant 'she.' Lara uses she." Or you can simply contribute to the conversation about Lara (assuming it's an appropriate conversation in the first place) while making sure to use lots of she/her pronouns.

- Later that week, George asks Lara if she's had "the surgery." Without speaking for Lara, you can give her an out by saying something like, "Gosh, George, that's a personal question. You know, Lara, I wouldn't blame you at all if you don't want to talk about that at work." Later, you can follow up with George to make sure he understands that gender identity is not defined by surgery, and that his question was inappropriate (and could be considered sexual harassment). You might remind him that he probably would never ask a cisgender coworker about a genital surgery they might have had, like a biopsy or a vasectomy. If George is curious about trans communities in general, you can offer him resources such as this book with which to educate himself.

- At the neighborhood block party, your neighbor Florence is musing about a TV program she saw about trans children. She says, "I would never let a boy of mine wear a dress to school. I just don't think kids that young can know if they'll grow up to be a transsexual." Choosing wisely among the dozen or so things you could challenge about that statement, you opt for the personal approach, and say, "Gosh Florence, that's hard for me to hear. I have some friends who are trans, and they've talked to me about how heartbreaking it was for them when people disbelieved them about their identities." From there, the tone of the conversation changes, and Florence is able to openly wonder about trans children, rather than make definitive, uninformed statements.

Most of the time, if you're lucky, the disrespectful talk you have to interrupt will be well-intentioned. Occasionally, you may encounter people expressing overt malice or ill will toward a trans person, or toward trans people in general. In between those two extremes, you may hear people expressing resentment that they are expected to change their behavior to show respect for a trans person, or declare their intentions to continuing behaving in hurtful ways.

How can you respond to such hostility? First of all, pay attention to your own safety. Part of being an ally is surviving to show up another day. Nobody wants you to get beat up or fired for getting into it with someone who isn't going to listen anyway. Second, consider your goal in responding. Are you trying to educate the person? To get them to consider another point of view? To just stop them from doing any more harm by continuing to talk that way in the moment? Or, is your main goal to educate bystanders who witness the incident? Having a clear goal will help you respond from a grounded, confident position. Finally, speak honestly from your own perspective (not speaking for someone else). It's often useful to open with a statement about feelings, such as "Wow, that's really hard to hear," and then provide a very small, digestible piece of information, like "I know some trans people, and it hurts me to hear them spoken about that way."

It's important to be aware of your own position when you respond to inappropriate comments. If you are cisgender, you are responding from a place of relative privilege. As daunting as it may be to approach such a conversation, consider how much harder it might be if the comments were targeting you. This kind of work is an especially crucial role for cisgender allies, because trans people who intervene in such conversations are often vulnerable to further harassment and violence. It's also important because trans people are a very small proportion of the population, and there just are not enough of us to educate the whole world, one person at a time!

As someone who has taken steps to become a better ally, you can serve as a model to people who may be struggling to understand (whether or not they acknowledge that struggle). Sometimes a statement of commonality, such as "It was confusing to me too at first, but once I started learning more about trans communities, I realized..." can go a long way.

A final tip: Be extremely cautious about using analogies. For some people, it can be useful to draw parallels between the oppression of trans people (sometimes called cissexism) and other systems such as racism, sexism, ableism and so on. But analogies are always imperfect, and can sometimes go horribly wrong. Make sure not to imply that cissexism is "just like" racism, or that being trans is the same as having a disability, or that your experience as a gay person automatically means you can "completely understand" what it's like to be trans.

> CISSEXISM: The system of oppression that privileges cisgender people while marginalizing trans people.

Practice: Responding to Ignorant or Hostile Comments

What ignorant or hostile comments about trans people have you heard? What kind of misgendering (calling someone the wrong gender) have you heard? If you can, make a list of specific things you've heard people say.

Then choose one example, and think through how you would respond:

1. Assess your safety in the situation.
2. Consider your goals
3. Consider your identities (gender, trans status, sexual orientation, race, ...) and how they might influence the conversation. What privileges do you bring to the interaction? In what way are you not privileged in the conversation?
4. Consider your relationship with the person who made the comment. What influence do you have with them? What commonalities can you draw on?

Finally, practice with a trusted friend! It really does get easier with practice. You can even write down all the comments you want to be able to respond to on slips of paper, and then take turns drawing them out of a hat and responding to them. The more comfortable you get with some options for responding, the more confidently you'll be able to speak up when the time comes.

Avoid Police

Trans people, especially trans women of color and those for whom strangers are likely to guess that they're trans, are extremely vulnerable to violence from police and to disproportionate arrest and incarceration. If you are used to thinking of police and other authority figures as helpers, remember that this is usually not the case for trans folks.

If you're with a trans friend and you encounter police (or even mall security), try not to draw attention, and calmly look for opportunities to exit the situation. If the two of you have to interact with the police, it may be helpful for you to do most of the talking. If your friend hasn't changed the name or gender on their id, it's probably helpful to avoid gendering them in front of police (for example, don't use any pronouns or their first name), in case they have to show id that would contradict what you just called them.

Of course, much of this depends on the specifics of the situation and of your and your friend's identities, including race, class, etc. as well as trans status. If you have a trans friend with whom you are often out in public, consider asking in advance how they'd like you to handle such a situation.

Offer Support for Medical Transition—And All Health Needs

Allies often show up after a trans person has had transition-related surgery to bring meals and help with household tasks while the person is healing. These surgeries are not always covered by insurance and can be very costly, so many people turn to crowdfunding to cover some or all of the costs (although crowdfunding is rarely as successful as people hope it will be). Showing up for post-surgery recovery support and contributing to a crowdfunding campaign can be helpful allyship roles, especially if the trans person is estranged from their family of origin, or their family of origin is far away, or doesn't have a lot of resources to share.

For many people, it may feel easier to support someone around transition-related medical care, compared to supporting people around other kinds of health needs. This could be because recovering from transition-related care is often a happy time. The assistance needed tends to be relatively simple and logistical, rather than the intense emotional labor that often comes with supporting someone during a health crisis. Another reason might be the mystique surrounding transition-related surgeries. People sometimes see medical transition as almost magically transformative, or as extremely unusual. They want to be involved in someone's recovery because they want to be part of that powerful, once-in-a-lifetime moment.

Even though this perspective can lead to supportive behavior, it is not the best place to be coming from as an ally. It prioritizes the helper's desires over the helpee's needs, and can impose meaning on a procedure that may not reflect what it means to the person having it. Remember that the experience of having transition surgeries is different for different people. Whatever you imagine the surgery might mean to someone, or whatever you know it would mean to you, may not be what it means to the person who is having it. It is totally normal and okay for someone having transition surgery to have a wide range of feelings around it, including joy, sadness, confusion, relief, some combination, or none of the above. Helpful allyship means trying to enter the situation with an open heart and mind, without needing the experience to mean anything in particular or feel any particular way.

Finally, when I see allies pour out of the woodwork to support a trans person after surgery, it gives me hope that our communities could learn to be as generous about other needs as well. Trans people, and all people, need community support for all kinds of health-related issues. If you have the capacity to help out with recovery after transition surgery, you can probably be just as helpful with less glamorous healthcare situations, like recovering from a hernia surgery, or managing an ongoing chronic illness. Whatever kind of support you are able to offer around healthcare situations, I urge you to offer it whenever you can and wherever it's needed, not only when the health issue is specifically related to your friend's trans-ness.

Reflection: Supporting Someone Around Medical Transition

The next time you offer support to support a trans person you know around transition-related care, first take some time to reflect on your own feelings about the situation. What, if anything, does this person's transition, or this particular step in their transition, mean to you? What does it mean to the person you're supporting, as far as you know? What do you need to do in order to set your own feelings aside, and support the person where they are at, rather than where you are at?

This can be an especially useful reflection for trans folks who are supporting other trans folks around transition-related care. For example, you may know what your surgery meant to you (or will mean to you), but your friend may be having the same surgery for a very different reason, or the experience may bring up very different feelings for them. Don't assume that you know what their experience will be.

If it feels appropriate to your relationship, you might ask the person what the procedure means to them; or, you might just support them without having to know.

Offer Support for Dealing with Binary Bureaucracies

So many systems are built on the assumption that trans people don't exist. Government benefits applications, health insurance, healthcare itself, hostels, shelters, gym locker rooms. Even shopping for clothes you'll encounter a men's section and a women's section. Teaming up to face such challenges together can make a world of difference. If you're cisgender, you may be able to use your privilege to and credibility to help your trans friend get what they need. If you're trans, you can both support each other to stay grounded and confident in your identity even if the system can't acknowledge it. Different kinds of support will be helpful to different people, so check in beforehand about what kind of allyship would be most appreciated.

In some cases, you may also be in a position to make a system a little more welcoming. Does your workplace need training on trans inclusion, or updated trans-inclusive intake forms? Work from the inside to make that happen! Does your gym have a suggestion box? Suggest that they create a gender-neutral bathroom so that people who need a little extra privacy (whether because of gender or for any other reason) can shower and change clothes safely.

Give Truly Positive Compliments

Well-meaning reactions to trans people's gender expressions can be almost as problematic as negative ones. "You look so good, I never would have guessed you were trans." "Wow, your makeup looks great today, I can't even tell that you have facial hair." Even though they are intended positively, these kinds of comments imply that all trans people want to look cisgender, that looking cisgender is the ultimate accomplishment for a trans person, and that the speaker is the ultimate authority on how "successful" the trans person's gender expression is. Whatever the intention, the impact is to reinforce cisgender privilege and devalue trans existence.

On the other hand, some people seem to never compliment their trans friend or coworker at all. Maybe they're too nervous about saying the wrong thing, or maybe they're just really uncomfortable with the fact of someone being trans.

Just like with any cisgender person, really allyship is conveyed in matching your honest compliments to what your trans friend needs and wants to hear. As a general rule, compliment things that people have control over—choices and behaviors, rather than body size, shape or parts. "Those earrings are so compelling, where did you find them?" "You did a fantastic job in that meeting this morning." "I really appreciate your sense of humor."

If someone specifically asks you for feedback on their gender expression—which will usually only happen if y'all are *very* close—you can give honest feedback while also reassuring them that they are okay just the way they are. If someone asks, "Is this outfit "passing" enough? Because I really want to look male for my job interview today," they're telling you that there is an important practical purpose for the question, and you can (and should) answer honestly. But also say your overall impression, not only related to passing. For example, "You look like a confident, professional guy. I think most people will read you as male, although people who have met trans guys might guess that you are one. You might want to touch up the ironing on that sleeve." Remember, this kind of feedback is useful *only* if it's specifically requested!

Be Discerning About Trans-related Media

Some people who are new to trans-allyship get so excited about it that they want to forward every trans-related news article they see to their one trans friend. Keep in mind that you are probably not the first person to have seen that article and forwarded it. Also, as noted in the Introduction, most trans-related media is oversimplified at best. It tends to reproduce one monolithic version of trans experience, too often reflects inaccurate and harmful stereotypes, and sometimes uses disrespectful or out-of-date terminology. Perhaps more importantly, trans people are whole people, and we want you to think of us when you read something we're interested in, not only something tangentially related to our genders.

Sometimes, people bring up trans people in media in ways that reinforce cisgender privilege. When a cisgender person says to a trans person, "Did you see that story about so-and-so's transition? Isn't she so inspiring? I really felt like I get it about the trans experience after hearing her interview," it may come across as, "Trans existence seems so impossible to me that just the mere fact of being trans is a heroic accomplishment. I don't really know or care what else that person may have accomplished in her life. Trans people's stories matter to the extent that cisgender people feel good about them. I've read one story, which mostly confirmed what I had already heard about trans experiences. Now I feel like I understand everything about trans experience, and I may not be open to hearing stories that complicate my understanding or help me see the vast variety of trans experience."

Instead, cultivate the ability to assess trans-related media. This goes back to the *analysis* skill discussed in Chapter 1. When you see trans-related coverage, you should be able to evaluate its accuracy, intended audience, and political implications before deciding whether your trans friend might appreciate receiving the link or being asked their opinion on it. This activity may help:

Activity: Trans Media Literacy

Look up one news story about a trans person (or just read the next one that comes across your Facebook feed). Ask yourself:

- Would there be a story here if the person wasn't trans?
- Is the person treated as a whole, real person? Are they demonized or lionized or exoticized?
- What details are included about the person's pre-transition past, their body, or their medical situation? (For example, are there pictures of the person before transition? Is a previous name used? Are medications and surgeries listed?) Are these details at all relevant to the content of the story?
- Does the story include stereotyped gender images, such as photos of a trans woman applying makeup or a trans man shaving his face?
- If there are "experts" cited in the story, are they trans people? Mental health professionals? Something else? What does the choice of expert imply about the author's view of trans communities?

- What, if any, claims does the article make about trans people in general? Which trans people are the claims true for, and which are they not true for? (Consider age, binary/nonbinary identities, transition status, race, class, gender identity, sexual orientation ...)
- Who is the intended audience of this story? How can you tell?
- What is the article trying to make you think and feel about trans people in general and/or this particular trans person?

Given all that, what unintentional messages might you be sending by sharing or bringing up this story with your trans friend?

If this activity is difficult at first, or if most media coverage about trans people seems fine to you, consider teaming up with another ally who may have more experience with this kind of analysis. Talking through a couple of articles or videos together may give you a new perspective.

SPECIAL ALLYSHIP SITUATIONS

Aside from your general allyship as a community member who cares, there are some special situations that require particular skills and resources for effective allyship. This isn't the place to cover all of them in depth, but here are some tips and starting places for parents of trans children, as well as professionals such as educators, case managers, therapists and medical providers.

For Parents of Trans Children

Parents of trans children have a unique dual role as not only allies but also parents. Practically speaking, the main difference is that you must sometimes be the "expert." Whereas in most allyship situations it's a safe bet the trans person you're supporting knows a lot more about their needs than you do, that may not be true of your child (especially young children). Parents of trans children need to strike a careful balance between following the child's lead as far as understanding their identity and needs, while also taking responsibility for providing information, resources, and guidance in an age-appropriate way.

Parents of trans kids often must become advocates with their kids' school, pediatrician, summer camps, and so on. This requires not only understanding your particular child's needs, but also negotiating about policies, accommodations, and messaging issues, as well as giving impromptu "trans 101" explanations and garnering support from key allies within these organizations.

Even though you will often be the first advocate for your child, keep in mind you shouldn't have to do it all alone or become a semi-professional advocate. It is generally inappropriate, for example, for your child's school to invite you to speak at an assembly or train their staff on trans inclusion. First of all, it can unfairly single out your family and child, positioning your child as the "problem," rather than recognizing the school's lack of preparedness to welcome trans students as problematic. Second, it puts a lot of responsibility on you to implement the "solution" of educating the community, rather than making the school responsible for fulfilling its own professional development needs. Finally, being an expert on your kid's current needs does not make you qualified to train an organization on trans inclusion generally. If you're put in such a situation, you can respectfully suggest that the organization hire one of the many skilled trans educators who have developed effective programs and professional development curricula for exactly this purpose (like me and my colleagues at Think Again Training).

Meanwhile, in the midst of supporting their child and advocating for appropriate treatment in school and elsewhere, parents are often navigating their own emotional process around their kid's identity and transition. Some parents go through a period of grieving, letting go of the hopes and expectations they may have attached to their child's assigned gender. Others may worry about what "caused" their child's transness, or about how relationships with friends, neighbors, or extended family may be impacted. All of these responses are normal and okay, as long as you're working through them appropriately, while you also support your child through their process.

The most important things for all parents of trans children to do is get the support they need for themselves. Peer support groups through PFLAG (an organization for family members of LGBTQ people) or various social media groups, support from a family therapist familiar with trans issues, and support from knowledgeable friends can all be helpful. You might also want to check out Rex Butt's book *Now What?: For Families with Trans and Gender-Nonconforming Children*. And, refer back to this book's section on Trans Children and Youth (pp. 27–30) for more information.

For Professionals

A professional's role in showing allyship to trans students, clients, or patients can range from fairly straightforward to enormously complex. On one end of the spectrum, it's as simple as treating the trans person as they want to be treated, including calling them the name, pronouns and other gendered words that they want to be called. As you've already read, this is important for every allyship situation, but as a professional it is particularly vital. When you accidentally call someone the wrong pronoun, it may not be the first time it happened that day—it may not even be the tenth time—and you are a person with professional authority who is supposed to be helping them. The effectiveness and outcomes of your professional relationship can be derailed by well-intentioned missteps. Your professional role makes it all the more important to get the basic allyship stuff right.

Professionals' potential allyship roles get more complex, and more effective, when you think beyond supporting one trans person at a time, and consider how you can integrate gender inclusion in your overall practice. This is important whether or not you know you are working with any trans people. It's important both because some trans people will not disclose that they're trans unless they see that it is safe to do so, and also because a broadly gender-inclusive environment improves things for everyone, not only trans people. This kind of broad gender-inclusive practice requires identifying ways in which your work may be guided by a binary assumption, and then re-imagining it in a way that includes all genders.

Beyond your individual practices, professionals should also pay attention to policies and structures that may hinder full trans inclusion in your organization. You've already read about supporting trans people in navigating binary bureaucracies. In your professional role, you may be working in one of those very bureaucracies that's causing so much difficulty. That puts you in an important position to help trans people navigate those policies to get what they need.

Being part of an organization also gives you an opportunity to become an internal advocate, to help transform, or at least reform, problematic policies. Taking your allyship to an organizational level can benefit not only the people currently impacted, but also all those who may interact with the organization in the future. As you learn more about your organization's strengths and weaknesses around trans inclusion, you may want to seek out training, consultation, or other resources to help move the organization toward best practices.

Finally, although the great majority of your allyship as a professional will likely consist of making the work you already do trans-inclusive and broadly gender-inclusive, there are some areas in which trans-specific expertise and skills will be necessary for you to be ready to serve trans people well. You may need to explore how information about trans people has been left out of your professional education, and take steps to educate yourself.

The sections below offer some more specific examples of allyship for educators, medical providers, and human service providers such as therapists and case managers. Keep in mind that these are just examples. Reading this book is not sufficient professional development to prepare you to do excellent work with trans folks in your professional role. As you take in these examples, you may discover areas in which you need further information or training. The resource list on p. 91 offers some places to begin the next steps in your self-education.

As you learn more about trans topics related to your work, you may be called on to educate your colleagues on trans inclusion. Like with parents, this usually should not be your role. Too often, an agency asks one of the most junior and/or marginalized staff members to provide diversity training—for free—to the rest of the staff. This is exploitative and often ineffective. Being the first to have a trans student in your class, having trans friends, or even being trans yourself does not necessarily make you qualified to provide such training. Even if you are qualified, you may want to consider bringing in an outside trainer, simply because adult learners often have an easier time taking advice from an "outside expert" than from a familiar colleague. Plus, you don't want to set yourself up for unnecessary conflict with colleagues who may be resistant to adopting trans inclusion practices. Taking all that into account, if you do happen to have pretty broad-based expertise on trans communities, have skills in adult education, and feel confident providing professional development training in your own workplace, you don't have to reinvent the wheel. You can seek out training resources from organizations like those listed in the resource list and from us here at Think Again Training.

Educators

• Call everyone the name and pronoun they want to be called.

• Whether or not you have any trans students, consider how your classroom practices might unnecessarily impose binary gender. Do you usually line students up in a girls' line and a boy's line? Mix it up! Do you address students as "ladies and gentlemen?" Instead try something more gender-neutral, like "students," "scholars," "friends," or just "everyone."

• Consider introducing group pronoun practices such as those described in Chapter 4, *with* age-appropriate explanation.

• Be prepared to educate and support students to understand and respect their trans peers' gender identities and transitions, including having clear policies on gender-based bullying and harassment.

• Learn the laws and policies related to gender and trans inclusion for your school. For example, some states have pretty strong laws or policies protecting the rights of public school students to express their gender identities in school—even if the parents are not supportive of their child's transition. In other states, no protection is in place, and laws may even make it harder for schools to support trans students as they'd like to. To fully support trans students, you should know what they can expect around issues like bathroom use, athletic participation, dress code, roommate assignment, name tags, forms/record keeping, and so on.

• Think about trans inclusion in the content you teach. If you teach literature or reading, do the books you use include any trans or gender-nonconforming characters? Get some that do! If you teach about health, from potty training all the way up to AP Biology and beyond, do you talk about bodies in a way that acknowledges a diversity of anatomy and gender experiences? Start! Every subject can be taught in a way that acknowledges and respects all genders.

Healthcare Providers

• Call everyone the name and pronoun they want to be called.

• When taking a medical history, make sure there are obvious and welcoming opportunities for trans people to give you information you might need about their bodies—for example, for a trans man to tell you that he is pregnant or for a trans woman to tell you she is due for a prostate exam. Even as a medical provider, you cannot always tell by looking if someone is trans, and they won't always tell you unless you show them that it will be safe and helpful to do so.

• Consider how you talk about patients' body parts, especially parts that might be experienced as gendered. Do you ask patients what words they like to use? Try asking! It can be uncomfortable for some trans people to hear their body parts referred to in gendered ways that don't reflect their gender identity. Identifying the language that will work best for each person can help you communicate more effectively and compassionately.

• Find out what options exist within current record keeping systems so that patients can indicate what name and pronoun they want to be called, and so that every staff member who interacts with the patient would have that information. If there is no good way to do this in the current system, find out what it would take to update the system.

• Learn the laws and policies related to gender and trans inclusion for your workplace and for healthcare in general (including insurance coverage). Learn about the work of trans rights organizations that are working to improve trans inclusion in healthcare policy, and learn from colleagues about workarounds that can help to maximize trans-inclusive care in the meanwhile.

• Familiarize yourself with the latest WPATH Standards of Care. Assess what services you are already qualified to provide, and what services you could be trained to provide. For example, primary care providers can provide transition-related hormone therapy for most patients with just a tiny bit of self-education.

WPATH: World Professional Association for Transgender Health.

• Consider your potential role as a "gatekeeper" with the power to approve or deny requests for hormones and surgeries. Familiarize yourself with the range of protocols that providers use to initiate transition services, including "informed consent," and clarify your own ethics and guidelines around respecting trans people's personal autonomy while recognizing the power you hold in the current system.

• Establish your network of referral resources, and learn how to vet them to make sure you understand what exactly they can provide and how trans-inclusive they really are.

Therapists and Other Human Service Professionals

- Call everyone the name and pronoun they want to be called.

- Whether or not you have any trans clients that you know of, consider how you talk about gender with all your clients. Are there ways in which your assumptions about "normal" women and men might discourage people from exploring or disclosing experiences outside that norm? Practice acknowledging the possibility of gender diversity in all your language. If you catch yourself saying stuff like "many women experience ...," to assure a woman client that her experience is normal, ask yourself if it would be equally true and helpful to say "many people experience...." This does not mean you should minimize the importance of gender for cisgender clients, but rather that you should double check whether the importance of gender in a particular conversation is coming from the client, or whether you are inserting it unintentionally through the language you use.

- For group settings, be prepared to educate and support clients to understand and respect their trans peers' gender identities and transitions, including having clear policies on gender-based bullying and harassment.

- Think about how the models you work from (diagnostic models, therapeutic models, human development models, etc.) make sense of trans experience. Do they acknowledge trans experience as part of normal human gender diversity, rather than pathologizing it as a mental health "problem" in itself? Look beyond professional resources about trans clients to familiarize yourself with contemporary trans communities from their own perspectives. Read trans authors, explore trans-led organization, and attend trans community events.

- For group setting, consider introducing group pronoun practices such as those described in Chapter 4, *with* context-appropriate explanation.

- Learn the laws and policies related to gender and trans inclusion for your field and your organization (including those related to health insurance coverage). Carefully distinguish between requirements and guidelines—not everything that gets handed down as a "rule" really is one. Learn about the work of trans rights organizations that are working to improve trans inclusion in healthcare policy, and learn from colleagues about workarounds that can help to maximize trans-inclusive care in the meanwhile.

- Consider your role as a "gatekeeper," with the power to certify someone's readiness to initiate transition-related medical care. Familiarize yourself with the latest WPATH Standard of Care and with the requirements of local providers from whom your trans clients might be seeking services. Seek support and clinical supervision from more experienced colleagues who have positive reputations in trans communities, and clarify your own ethics around respecting trans people's personal autonomy while recognizing the power you hold in the current system.
- Establish your network of referral resources, and learn how to vet them to make sure you understand what exactly they can provide and how trans-inclusive they really are.

Keep it Going!

Congratulations! By reading this far, you are already practicing your commitment to do right by the trans folks in your life. Of course, no reading or exercise can flip a magic switch to make allyship easy, or to undo all the counterproductive messages we've all been taught to believe about gender. But your honest reflection and practice will help you move in the world with integrity as a good friend and a reliable ally.

You probably realize by now that this book has only scratched the surface of what you could learn and do in allyship to trans people. Developing your allyship is a never-ending process. Keep thinking and reflecting. Stay in touch with your accountability networks. Consider generating some broader conversations around allyship in your community, through shared reading, discussion, events or training. However you choose to move forward with this work, I hope the tools you've learned here will prove helpful in approaching your allyship thoughtfully and well.

Finally, remember that the thinking you've done with this book is mostly about allyship to individual trans people—not to whole trans communities or movements. If you're interested in becoming an advocate for trans liberation at a systemic level, you can start by exploring and supporting the work of some of the organizations mentioned in the resource list, along with looking up your local trans organizations and community groups.

Resources

TRANS RIGHTS ORGANIZATIONS WHOSE WORK YOU SHOULD KNOW

- Audrey Lorde Project (NYC) – http://alp.org/
- Basic Rights Oregon – www.basicrights.org/
- Brown Boi Project – http://www.brownboiproject.org/
- COLAGE resources for kids of trans parents – http://www.colage.org/resources/kot/
- FORGE (Milwaukee, WI) – http://forge-forward.org/
- Gender Justice League (WA State) – www.genderjusticeleague.org/
- Global Action for Trans Equality – http://transactivists.org/
- InterACT – http://interactyouth.org/
- Mass Trans Political Coalition (MA) – http://www.masstpc.org/
- National Center for Transgender Equality – http://transequality.org/
- National Gay and Lesbian Task Force – http://www.thetaskforce.org/issues/transgender
- PFLAG trans family resources – http://community.pflag.org/transgender
- SONG (Southerners On New Ground) – http://southernersonnewground.org/
- Sylvia Rivera Law Project (NYC) – http://www.srlp.org/
- TGEU (Europe) – http://tgeu.org/
- TGI Justice Project (CA) – http://www.tgijp.org/
- Trans Justice Funding Project – https://www.transjusticefundingproject.org/
- Trans Faith – http://www.transfaithonline.org/
- Transgender Law & Policy Institute – http://www.transgenderlaw.org/
- Transgender Law Center (CA) – http://www.transgenderlawcenter.org/
- TransLatina Network – http://www.translatinanetwork.org/
- Trans People of Color Coalition – http://www.transpoc.org/
- Trans Student Education Resources – http://www.transstudent.org/
- WPATH (World Professional Association of Transgender Health Professionals) – http://www.wpath.org/

BOOKS, BLOGS, ZINES AND ARTICLES

Rex Butt's book, *Now What?: For Families with Trans and Gender-Nonconforming Children* (2013)

Eli Clare's books, *Brilliant Imperfection: Grappling with Cure* (2017), and *Exile & Pride: Disability, Queerness, and Liberation* (2015)

Finn Enke's book, *Transfeminist Perspectives in & Beyond Transgender & Gender Studies* (2012), especially Chapter 4, "The Education of Little Cis: Cisgender and the Discipline of Opposing Bodies"

Anne Fausto-Sterling's book, *Sex/Gender: Biology in a Social World* (2012)

Genderqueer.me "Featured Voices" blog – www.genderqueer.me/featured-voices

Assigned Male comics, by Sophie Labelle – www.facebook.com/assignedmale

Arlene Lev's book for therapists, *Transgender Emergence: Therapeutic Guidelines for Working with Gender-Variant People and Their Families* (2004)

Barbara Love's essay, "Developing a Liberatory Consciousness," in *Readings for Diversity and Social Justice*, 3nd ed. (2013), edited by Adams, Blumenfeld, Castañeda, Hackman, Peters, & Zúñiga

Gerald Mallon and Teresa Decrescenso's book for social workers, *Social Work Practice with Transgender and Gender-Variant Youth* (2009)

Mia McKenzie's book, *Black Girl Dangerous* (2014), and the blog she curates by the same name – www.bgdblog.org

Kai Minosh's essay on the Black Girl Dangerous blog, "Why Non-Natives Appropriating 'Two-Spirit' Hurts" – www.bgdblog.org/2016/07/appropriating-two-spirit

Janet Mock's book, *Redefining Realness* (2014)

Serena Nanda's book, *Gender Diversity: Cross-Cultural Variations* (2000)

Julia Serano's book, *Whipping Girl: A Transsexual Woman on Sexism and the Scapegoating of Femininity* (2009)

Dean Spade's book, *Normal Life: Administrative Violence, Critical Trans Politics, and the Limits of the Law* (2015)

Susan Stryker's book, *Transgender History* (2008)

PROFESSIONAL DEVELOPMENT RESOURCES

For Educators

- GLSEN – www.glsen.org
- GSA Network – www.gsanetwork.org
- Gender Spectrum – www.genderspectrum.org
- Trans Student Educational Resources – www.transstudent
- Trainings with Think Again Training – www.thinkagaintraining.com

For Mental Health and Other Human Service Providers

- Smith College School for Social Work's Trans and Gender-nonconforming resource page – www.smith.edu/ssw/tgnc
- Smith College School for Social Work's continuing education programs – www.smith.edu/ssw/continuing-education-participants
- TIGRIS Institute (offers online clinical supervision) – www.tigrisinstitute.com
- WPATH SOC – www.wpath.org
- Trainings with Think Again Training – www.thinkagaintraining.com

For Healthcare Providers

- Project Health (offers online clinical consultations for medical providers) – www.project-health.org/about-project-health
- UCSF Center of Excellence for Transgender Health – www.transhealth.ucsf.edu
- WPATH SOC – www.wpath.org
- Trainings with Think Again Training – www.thinkagaintraining.com

GLOSSARY

Language about trans identities and experiences is constantly evolving, and different people may use these terms in different ways. A more extensive (and regularly updated) glossary is available at www.thinkagaintraining.com.

Gender and Sexual Orientation Concepts

ALLYSHIP (n.): Informed, accountable action that contributes to other people's ability to survive and thrive in a context of inequality.

BIOLOGICAL SEX (n.): Sex refers to one's body—the physiological and anatomical characteristics of maleness and femaleness with which a person is born or that develop with physical maturity. Biological sex markers include internal and external reproductive organs, chromosomes, hormone levels, and secondary sex characteristics such as facial hair and breasts. See also *Sex assigned at birth.*

CISSEXISM (n.): The system of oppression that privileges cisgender people while marginalizing trans people. Also sometimes called cisgenderism or transgender oppression.

INTERSECTIONALITY (n.): A way of thinking about how social identities (race, gender and so on) are inseparable and experienced simultaneously, as well as about how systems like racism, sexism, classism, ableism and so on are entangled and reinforce each other. Originally coined by Black feminist Dr. Kimberle Crenshaw.

MISPRONOUNING (v.): Calling someone the wrong pronoun, whether intentionally or unintentionally. For example, calling someone he when she wants to be referred to as she.

GENDER EXPRESSION (n.): Appearance and behaviors that convey something about one's gender identity, or that others interpret as conveying something about one's gender identity, including clothing, mannerisms, communication patterns, etc.

GENDER IDENTITY (n.): People's own understandings of themselves in terms of gendered categories, like man and woman, boy and girl, transgender, genderqueer, and many others. Gender identity cannot be observed; the only way you can know someone's gender identity is if they tell you. Some people's gender identity is consistent for their whole lives; other people experiences shifts in their gender identity over time.

PASSING (v., adj.): Being seen as belonging unquestionably to a particular group, e.g. being seen as a woman or as a man. Often, it refers to a trans person being seen as the gender they are; occasionally it refers to being seen as the gender that one wants to be seen as at the moment, for safety or other reasons. Some people use "passing" specifically to mean being seen as cisgender (e.g. a trans woman who is assumed by others to be a cisgender woman is "passing"), while for others it is not that specific. Passing is a very complex and problematic concept, not only with regard to trans issues but also in terms of race, class, and other systems of categorization and power. Useful thoughts on some of the problems with "passing" can be found in Julia Serano's *Whipping Girl* (Chapter 8).

SEX ASSIGNED AT BIRTH (n.): The sex category (almost always male or female) assigned to each of us on ID documents, beginning with the birth certificate.

SEXUAL ORIENTATION (n.): An individual's patterns of romantic and/or sexual attraction, in terms of gender. For example, someone may be attracted to people of the same gender as themself, to people of a particular other gender, or to people of all genders. Sexual orientation is not the same as gender expression or gender identity. People of any gender may have any sexual orientation.

TRANSITION (n., v.): Any of the medical, social, legal, spiritual and personal processes that a trans person may go through in order to live their life in a way that works for their gender.

Identity Categories

AG (adj., n.): Pronounced like A.G., short for aggressive. Identity term embraced by some masculine/butch African American lesbians.

AGENDER (adj.): Describes someone who identifies as having no gender, as genderless or gender-free.

ASEXUAL (adj., n.): Someone who experiences little or no sexual attraction. (Note this is about sex as in sexuality and sexual orientation, not sex as in biological sex.) Sometimes shortened to ace (adj., n.).

BUTCH (adj., n.): Refers to several particular kinds of queer masculinity, especially in lesbian and gay male communities (however, the qualities that define butch are not identical in lesbian communities as in gay male communities). Butches tend to occupy particular roles within the gender dynamics of a queer scene, often (but *not* exclusively) in relation to femmes. These roles are flexible and evolving, and also highly specific to place and time.

CISGENDER (adj.): Non-trans. From a Latin prefix meaning "on the same side," as opposed to trans- which means "across." Describes people whose gender identity matches what is expected of them in their culture based on their sex assigned at birth—e.g. people assigned male at birth who identify as men and people assigned female at birth who identify as women.

CROSSDRESSER (n.): A person who enjoys dressing in clothes typically associated with the other of the two socially sanctioned genders. Most cross dressers are heterosexual men who enjoy wearing women's clothes occasionally. (An older term for the same group is transvestites, which is now broadly considered disrespectful.)

DRAG KINGS & DRAG QUEENS (n.): Drag is the practice of dressing and acting in an exaggerated masculine or feminine way, usually playfully and for theatrical performance. Drag Queens are usually men whose performances highlight femininity; Drag Kings are usually women whose performances highlight masculinity. People with nonbinary gender identities can also do drag; e.g. a genderqueer person whose drag performance highlights masculinity can be a drag king.

ENBY (adj., n.): Also "nb," short for nonbinary. Anyone whose gender identity does not fit into either of the two culturally accepted gender categories (men and women). (Does not include most trans women and trans men, who although trans, do have a gender identity as a man or a woman.) A relatively new term that is coming to be used as an umbrella term, encompassing people who may identify as genderqueer, gender-fluid, agender, and more.

FA'AFAFINE (n.): In traditional Samoan culture, a male-assigned person who is raised like a girl and taught to fulfill traditional women's roles. Fa'afafine are considered a distinct gender group, "like" women but not exactly women.

FEMME (adj., n.): Refers to several particular kinds of queer femininity, especially in lesbian and gay male communities (however, the qualities that define femme are not identical in lesbian communities as in gay male communities). Femmes tend to occupy particular roles within the gender dynamics of a queer scene, often (but *not* exclusively) in relation to butches. These roles are flexible and evolving, and also highly specific to place and time.

FEY (adj.): Literally referring to fairies, fey describes a particular kind of playful or whimsical feminine gender expression in some gay men.

GENDER-FLUID (adj.): Having a fluid gender identity (not only expression). Describes someone whose gender identity may regularly shift from week to week, day to day, or within a day.

GENDERQUEER (adj.): One of many identity labels used by trans people whose gender identity does not fit into either of the two culturally accepted gender categories (men and women). Genderqueer means different things to different people, and genderqueer people look, act and describe themselves in a wide variety of ways. However, genderqueer is not an umbrella term; you should only refer to someone as genderqueer if you know that they want to be described that way.

HIJRA (adj., n.): In South Asia, the most common of several traditional gender categories beyond man and woman. Hijras are either intersex or assigned male at birth, have traditionally feminine gender expression, and occupy social and religious roles specific to hijra. Hijras are mentioned in religious texts dating back thousands of years, and today the category is recognized by federal governments in Nepal, Bangladesh, India and Pakistan. Nevertheless, as a group hijras are economically marginalized.

INTERSEX (adj.): Describes someone whose anatomy or physiology is not easily categorized as simply male or female. This may be noticed at birth, or may not be apparent until puberty. Some intersex people are also trans, and many others are not. For more information regarding intersexuality, see http://interactyouth.org/

LESBIAN (adj., n.): Women whose primary romantic and/or erotic attraction is to other women.

MACHA (adj., n.): Identity term embraced by some butch/masculine Latinas.

MUXE (n.): In traditional Zapotec culture, a male-assigned person who takes on some of the roles traditional to women, sometimes but not always including dressing in women's clothes. Muxes may marry women or men, and in either case are not considered homosexual since they are considered to be their own category, and neither women or men.

NONBINARY (adj.): As a general descriptor, can refer to anything that has more than two categories. As an identity term, describes individuals whose gender identity is neither man nor woman but rather both, neither, and/or something else, including those who might identify more specifically as genderqueer, agender, gender-fluid, and many more.

QUEEN (n.): Identity term embraced by some gay men who embody a particular queer femininity (not restricted to drag queens).

QUEER (adj., n.): An umbrella term describing a wide range of people who do not conform to heterosexual and/or gender norms; a reclaimed derogatory slur taken as a political term to unite people who are marginalized because of their nonconformance to dominant gender identities and/or heterosexuality. Sometimes used as a shortcut for LGBT. Other times used to distinguish politically queer people from more mainstream LGBT people. Because of its origin as a derogatory slur, this term should be used thoughtfully. If you're not queer, or for public communications, LGBT is often more appropriate.

STUD (n.): Identity term embraced by some masculine/butch African American lesbians.

TRANS / TRANSGENDER / TRANS* (adj.): Commonly used in at least two pretty different ways, so it's useful to clarify how you are using it for a given conversation:

1. Describes anyone whose gender identity and/or gender expression differs significantly from what is expected of them in their culture based on their sex assigned at birth. This broad category includes transgender(2), transsexual and genderqueer people, cross dressers, drag queens and kings, masculine women and feminine men, and more. We use the term so broadly because it enables us to talk about challenges and barriers facing the whole range of trans people—but it's important to remember that not everyone who could be described as trans in this definition self-identifies as a trans person.

   "Trans" is most commonly used in this way, although you will hear it used as (2) as well.) When used this way, trans is sometimes spelled with an asterisk: trans*. The asterisk is meant as a reminder that the intention is to include *everyone* who could possibly be described as trans, not just a particular subset of trans people, such as (2). Using the asterisk was very popular, although not universal, from about 2012–2015. Since then it has begun to fall out of favor, with some trans folks finding its impact actually more exclusionary than just using "trans" and meaning it broadly.

2. Describes anyone who has an experience of transitioning (socially, legally and/or medically) from living as one gender to living as another gender. Includes transgender women, transgender men, and many people with nonbinary gender identities. Does not include those whose gender expression, *but not* gender identity, differ from what's expected of them (such as masculine women and feminine men).

"Transgender" is more commonly used in this way, although you will hear it used as (1) as well. Tip: in Standard English, transgender should always be used as an adjective. As a noun (e.g. "she's a transgender") or past tense verb ("transgendered") it sounds disrespectful to many.

TRANSFEMININE (adj.): Usually used to describe trans people who are assigned male at birth and whose identity is more like woman than like man, including transgender women as well as some people with nonbinary gender identities. Some people find the term problematic because "feminine" typically refers to gender expression, not identity; therefore, the term can be seen as excluding trans women who express themselves in more masculine ways (or just are not particularly feminine), and reinforcing the idea that trans women must have feminine gender expression in order to be taken seriously as women or as part of the transfeminine spectrum. Additionally, the term implies an assumption that man and woman are on a linear spectrum of gender identities, as if all gender identities can be measured in terms of their relative distance from the two binary standards, which does not reflect the understanding of many people with nonbinary identities. Transfeminine was coined as a less problematic alternative to MtF; obviously, it is still not perfect.

TRANSMASCULINE (adj.): Usually used to describe trans people who are assigned female at birth and whose identity is more like man than woman, including transgender men as well as some people with nonbinary gender identities. Some people find the term problematic because "masculine" typically refers to gender expression, not identity; therefore, the term can be seen as excluding trans men who express themselves through in more feminine ways (or just are not particularly masculine) and reinforcing the idea that trans men must have masculine gender expression in order to be taken seriously as men or as part of the transmasculine spectrum. Additionally, the term implies an assumption that man and woman are on a linear spectrum of gender identities, as if all gender identities can be measured in terms of their relative distance from the two binary standards, which does not reflect the understanding of many people with nonbinary identities. Transmasculine was coined as a less problematic alternative to FtM; obviously, it is still not perfect.

TRANSSEXUAL (adj., n.): Usually, a person who experiences an intense, persistent, and long-term feeling that their body and assigned sex are at odds with their gender identity. Such individuals often (but not always) desire to change their bodies to bring then into alignment with their gender identities. This term originated as a medical diagnosis, and many people do not identify with it for that reason.

TRANS MAN (or transgender man, or transsexual man) (n.): Someone assigned female at birth who now identifies and lives as a man. Also FTM/ F2M/ FtM (adj.): Female-to-Male, or Female-toward-Male, trans person. This latter is less used, because it emphasizes transition and/or assigned sex rather than current identity, and can be seen as disrespectful.

TRANS WOMAN (or transgender woman, or transsexual woman) (n.): Someone assigned male at birth who now identifies and lives as a woman. Also MTF/ M2F/ MtF (adj.): Male-to-Female, or Male-toward-Female, trans person. This latter is less used, because it emphasizes transition and/or assigned sex rather than current identity, and can be seen as disrespectful.

TRAVESTI (n., adj.): In Brazil and some other South American countries, a reclaimed term describing people assigned male at birth with feminine gender expression who occupy a particular gender role beyond man or woman. Also sometimes used more broadly to encompass trans women and other transfeminine people in these contexts. (Note this is not the same word or category as the English transvestite; see Crossdresser.)

TWO SPIRIT (adj.): Any of many gender categories beyond man and woman recognized in various Native American and First Nations cultures. Although you may hear some non-indigenous people self-identify as Two Spirit, this is a form of cultural appropriation. Many indigenous communities find it offensive and harmful to the communities where the terms originate for people outside those cultures to claim the term. Kai Minov's essay on the *Black Girl Dangerous* blog, "Why Non-Natives Appropriating 'Two-Spirit' Hurts," provides a really important perspective on this.

ABOUT THINK AGAIN TRAINING

Think Again Training helps schools, human services providers, workplaces and communities to:

- develop *critical consciousness* about issues of oppression and social justice
- gain *skills* to enact justice in our work and in our lives
- engage in informed and compassionate *dialogue* across differences
- work together *effectively and joyfully*

Our educational design and facilitation services include workshops, in-depth training retreats, small-group process facilitation and training of trainers. We also offer organizational assessments, problem-solving consultation and policy development. Some areas of special focus include gender diversity, trans inclusion, economic inequality, cross-class communication, intersectionality, and skill building for allyship.

Find out more at www.thinkagaintraining.com, or contact us at davey@thinkagaintraining.com to inquire about scheduling a training.

ABOUT THE AUTHOR

Davey Shlasko, M.Ed., founder of Think Again Training, has been writing, teaching and consulting around social justice issues since 2000. Davey has co-authored the chapters on Transgender Oppression, Classism, and Ableism for various editions of Teaching for Diversity and Social Justice. Davey is also a Marta Sotomayor Fellow and adjunct faculty member at Smith College School for Social Work.

ABOUT THE ILLUSTRATOR

Kai Hofius is a poet, illustrator, and full stack web developer-in-training. You can find more of their work at www.kaihofi.us

Design by Sophie Argetsinger—www.sophieargetsinger.com

CPSIA information can be obtained
at www.ICGtesting.com
Printed in the USA
LVHW070036010819
626115LV00020B/253/P

9 780990 636915